# STAN T[
# PRACTICAL GUIDE TO
# SOLO MINISTRY

# Stan Toler's Practical Guide to Solo Ministry

## How Your Church Can Thrive When You Lead Alone

### Stan Toler

wesleyan
publishing
house

Indianapolis, Indiana

Copyright © 2008 by Wesleyan Publishing House
Published by Wesleyan Publishing House
Indianapolis, Indiana 46250
Printed in the United States of America
ISBN 978-0-89827-383-0

Library of Congress Cataloging-in-Publication Data

Toler, Stan.
  Stan Toler's practical guide to solo ministry : how your church can
thrive when you lead alone.
     p. cm.
  ISBN 978-0-89827-383-0
  1. Pastoral theology. I. Title.
  BV4011.3.T645 2008
  253--dc22

                                                2008037326

This book contains general guidance and information regarding counseling
and related legal matters. It does not provide professional or legal counsel.
Readers are encouraged to consult with a mental health professional or
attorney regarding specific questions and concerns.

To Norman Wilson and Earle Wilson, two minister brothers
who have given their entire lives to the work
of the Kingdom and have influenced my life greatly.
You are among my heroes of the faith.

# CONTENTS

# PREFACE

When you look in the mirror first thing each morning, do you see the entire staff of your church staring back at you? If so, this book is for you, solo pastor. You and I know there's nothing else in this world that's quite like being the only pastor on staff at a congregation. That's why I wanted to follow up my earlier book, *Stan Toler's Practical Guide for Pastoral Ministry*, with a volume specifically for solo pastors, the book you're holding in your hands.

The solo pastor is required to be a true generalist: skilled in organizational management, leadership, volunteer recruitment, pastoral care, leading worship, preaching, raising money, and many other areas. If it's going to get done, everyone knows who'll make it happen. The message of this book is that solo pastors can experience joy, satisfaction, and success in their ministry, while making a significant difference for God's kingdom.

When I lead seminars, I often make the statement "It's not about theory, it's about practice." Never is that more true than in solo pastoral ministry. It's also an accurate description of my approach to ministry in general—and the contents of this book. I will certainly share big ideas and overarching principles. But most important are the practical tips that will help you put the principles into practice right away.

For this practical guide, I've chosen to focus on the ten
ministry areas that solo pastors seem to struggle with the most.
In each chapter, we'll begin by exploring the issues and challenges solo pastors face. Then, we'll examine any examples or
principles from Scripture that shed light on those issues and
challenges. Next, we'll identify the leadership principles that
provide a framework for effectively addressing that particular
ministry area. Finally, we'll look at some practical guidelines
that solo pastors can use to put those principles into practice
right away. As a bonus, you'll find a list at the end of each chapter
of next steps you can take to begin to apply what you've learned
in the chapter.

Throughout this book, I hope you'll sense the deep respect and
admiration I have for those of you on the front lines of ministry as
solo pastors. My goal is to encourage and equip you for the unique
and significant ministry God has given you. I hope you'll consider
me part of your team. Together we can do it.

STAN TOLER

# ACKNOWLEDGMENTS

Many thanks to the team at Wesleyan Publishing House, especially Don Cady, Lawrence W. Wilson, Kevin Scott, Joe Jackson, Rachael Stevenson, and Lyn Rayn. Thanks also to Ron McClung for editorial assistance, and to Deloris Leonard, and Pat Diamond. Thank you for helping me elevate this project to a new level.

# 1

# ADMINISTRATION
## Getting Organized for Ministry

*Effective solo pastors learn to manage their day
rather than letting it manage them.*

A herd of longhorn cattle may have been a common sight in downtown Kansas City in the nineteenth century. But a cattle stampede in the city streets—in 1997?

It wasn't meant to happen that way. Mike Murphy's downtown cattle drive was to be an orderly parade, with hundreds of spectators enjoying a nostalgic re-creation of the old-time cattle drives of the mid 1800s.

But then a lone steer broke from the herd and started toward a crowd of about two hundred

The difference between a mob and an army is organization.
—Author Unknown

parade watchers. Soon after, the rest of the 103 longhorns managed to surge past their wranglers. Five steers made for the glass doors of the Jones Store. Another fifty veered into a parking garage. At one intersection, a lone traffic cop valiantly

Communicate frequently but on your schedule. Concentrated uninterrupted work time is very important. I only return e-mails at two preset times a day so that I'm not disturbed by them or constantly wondering who has e-mailed you.

signaled for the herd to turn and stay on the planned route.

It didn't work.

The mortified cowboys, along with five motorcycle policemen, worked tirelessly to round up the cattle and restore order. Finally, a wrangler lassoed the last steer and tied him to a parking meter—on the eighth floor of the parking garage. Cowboy Matt Wansing explained, "We had them under control in the pen before the parade, and in the pen after the parade was done. In between, they were in charge."[1]

Does that describe your typical day? You start out in firm control of your schedule and time. But somewhere between sunrise and sunset, your best-laid plans stray into dimly lit parking garages, and the only option is to round them up and try again another day.

## Wrangling with Organization

It's easy for a pastor's day to go awry. You sit down to do some serious sermon preparation, and the phone rings—a children's worker calling to tell you she's ill. Her assistant is out of town, so will you please find someone else to lead children's church on Sunday?

Before getting back to sermon preparation you check your e-mail. Sure enough, twenty-three messages are parked there, waiting for your response. Several are junk mail, but eight require a personal answer. You take time to look up some Scripture verses to send to a parishioner struggling with cancer.

Before you finish responding to e-mails, another parishioner calls. Her husband has fallen and needs help getting up. She can't locate any of her children, the neighbors all seem to be gone, and she is desperate for help. Yes, she has called 9-1-1, but it would mean so much if you could come and have prayer with them.

When you return from your errand of mercy, your voice mail light is on; three new messages.

And on it goes. At the end of the day, you collapse into an armchair, muttering to yourself, "I didn't even touch my sermon!"

As a solo pastor, you may always feel a bit like you're herding cattle and rounding up strays, but you can learn to bring focus to your ministry and accomplish more of what God's given you to do and still have time left to spend with your family and friends. The key is to organize more effectively. Notice that I didn't say you need to organize flawlessly or exquisitely.

My secretary knows that I only return phone calls during certain hours each day so that I'm not at the disposal of everyone else's schedule. The secretary informs people in advance so that they can count on a response. But they also come to value my time.

When it comes to organization, every little bit of improvement helps. The more you organize, the more time you'll have available to accomplish your goals in every area of life.

The good news is that it's a skill anyone can become proficient in with effort. Your personal time management system may never win you worldwide fame, but it can make a significant difference in your life and ministry, and that's what counts.

Later in the chapter, I'll offer a number of principles for organizing your ministry, along with practical ideas for applying them. First, though, let's look at what Scripture has to say about organization.

## Organization in the Bible

Isaiah tells us that "the LORD is a God of justice" (Isa. 30:18). That verse might seem off topic in a chapter on organization, but actually the Hebrew word translated *justice* in this passage means "method, order, system, law." Sir George Adam Smith explained: "It is a great truth that the Almighty and All-merciful is the All-methodical too. No religion is complete in its creed, or healthy in its influence, which does not insist equally on all these."[2]

Creation itself demonstrates that we serve a God of order. The planets all revolve around the sun in a predictable pattern. The arrangement of the stars and the rotation of the earth are so predictable, navigators can sail ships and fly spacecraft by orienting themselves to these pinpoints of light. It's no wonder then that God's people have so much to gain from becoming organized.

Moses could identify with today's busy solo pastor. He felt overwhelmed too. For hours each day, he listened to people's complaints and mediated their conflicts. Even then, he didn't have time to hear them all. One day Moses' father-in-law, Jethro, witnessed the never-ending stream of people needing to talk to Moses. Later, Jethro took him aside and urged him to appoint judges to help him decide cases for the people. Otherwise,

Jethro warned him, "You and these people who come to you will only wear yourselves out" (Ex. 18:18). Like Moses, many solo pastors are completely worn out. One of the reasons is inefficient organization.

In just fifty-two days, Nehemiah led his people to rebuild the walls of Jerusalem, an incredible feat (Neh. 6:15). While he certainly enjoyed God's help and protection during the rebuilding process, Nehemiah also did a masterful job of organizing people for the job. He divided up the work, assigning to people portions of the wall that were nearest to their homes. He involved everyone in the work. Even the goldsmiths and perfume makers—not exactly construction worker types—contributed to the project. Nehemiah's superb organizational plan made it happen.

The apostles learned to organize better when the Greek-speaking Jews complained that their widows were being neglected in the daily distribution of food. Was there real neglect or was it a perception? We can't be sure, but we do know the apostles' workload was already at its limit. To prevent this problem from dividing the church and to prevent themselves from being burned out, the apostles appointed laypersons to handle these humanitarian needs. The apostles could then devote themselves to prayer and the ministry of the Word (Acts 6:1–6).

Jesus accomplished his earthly mission in a relatively short period of time. Amazingly though, he never seemed to be in a hurry. He was never anxious or agitated when others around him demanded his time. Yet he could say to the Father, "I have finished the work which You have given Me to do" (John 17:4 NKJV). While he always had time for others, he didn't allow their demands to dominate his schedule.

> The daily quiet time is like a shower. It washes, refreshes and renews. It protects us from the moral pollution that surrounds us. It prepares us to engage in the spiritual struggle that exists on every side.
>
> —George Sweeting

For example, when Lazarus was gravely ill, Mary and Martha called for Jesus to come quickly. He didn't. Four days later when Jesus arrived, Lazarus had already died. Martha and Mary both challenged him, "Lord, if you had been here, my brother would not have died" (John 11:21, 32). Jesus ignored their thinly veiled rebuke, making no apology for the delay. But neither did he lack compassion. Moments later, seeing their grief, he was overcome with emotion and wept (John 11:33, 35). He moved at his own pace.

In the boat on the Sea of Galilee, while the disciples were frantic with fear, Jesus slept in the stern. Waking him, they cried, "Teacher, don't you care if we drown?" (Mark 4:38). In other words, "Where are your priorities? People are suffering here and about to die!" Jesus, completely free of anxiety and any sense of compulsion, calmed the wind, soothed the waves, and confronted their lack of faith. He moved at his own pace.

## Keys to Better Organization

You too can apply key organizational principles to focus your efforts and help your congregation accomplish more enduring results for God's kingdom.

### Spend Time with God

As you think about organizing your work in ministry, your first priority will be to spend time with God so that you understand as best you can what he might want to accomplish through your life and ministry. Don't make the mistake that many people do of creating an elaborate plan and then asking God if that sounds fine to him. Study and meditate on Scripture, seek spiritual counsel, and cover your ministry in prayer. Only then are you ready to set goals, establish priorities, and create plans. If our lives and ministries are to be ordered and organized around God's priorities, we must first take time to sit at his feet and seek his heart.

The foundation for all this is your regular, consistent, and submissive walk with Christ. As Billy Graham reminds us, "Nothing can take the place of a daily devotional life with Christ."[3]

God has a plan for your life and ministry, and the best way to guarantee that his plan becomes reality is to regularly spend time with God, seeking to understand his heart and will for your life. Through our daily devotional life, we discipline ourselves to acknowledge God, to express our dependence on him, and to make his priorities our priorities.

> In reading the lives of great men, I found that the first victory they won was over themselves . . . self-discipline with all of them came first.
>
> —Harry S. Truman

Never allow yourself to become so busy that you don't have time to spend with God. Hudson Taylor, the great missionary, said, "Never mind how great the pressure is—only where the pressure lies. Never let it come between you and the Lord. Then the greater the pressure, the more it presses you to his heart."

## Focus On the Essentials

Solo pastors typically have lengthy to-do lists, including items they personally want to accomplish as well as items others thrust upon them. The problem with to-do lists, though, is that many times they're filled with low-priority, nonessential tasks. Jim Collins recommends developing a "stop doing list."[4] This is a list of tasks someone else can do. Or perhaps they don't need to be done at all.

Chuck Swindoll once made a list of things he cannot do. The list includes the following:

- Control anyone or everything.
- Change people or "fix" them.
- Explain everything that happens.
- Meet most people's expectations.
- Avoid tough decisions.
- Worry about who gets credit for what.
- Cling to the past.
- Do ministry alone.[5]

You can make your own list and it will be specific to you and your challenges.

Of course, if you delegate some of the things you can't do, you'll need to spend some time coaching and following up with the individuals to make sure they complete the job with excellence. But in the long run, you'll save time and give others an opportunity to grow and use their gifts in ministry.

## Invest in People

Although Ephesians 4:12 says the pastor's role is to "pre-pare God's people for works of service," the truth is that many solo pastors are so busy ministering they never get around to training others to do ministry.

Alan Nelson points out, "Churches are filled with immature Christians, not so much because of inadequate preaching, but because of a lack of equipping."[6]

Sue Mallory, author of *The Equipping Church*, says, "I think pastors have inherited the culture of 'the one-man band,' where the pastor is the 'doer of all significant things.'"[7]

If we buy in to that culture, we will always limit the effectiveness of our church. The ceiling will always be what the pastor alone can do. On the other hand, like the fishermen in my home state of West Virginia, if you string a line across the river with a lot of hooks on it, you will catch more fish than if you sit on the river bank and throw one line in the water. In some places that practice is illegal, but a lot of fish have wound up in frying pans that way. The good news? It is not illegal, in fact it is extremely wise, to invest in people by equipping them to do ministry. In so doing, you put many hooks in the water.

It takes time to train laypersons. And, frankly, most of us, especially gifted preachers, would rather prepare sermons than equipping sessions for laypeople. But, while I would never

> Keep in mind that you are always saying no to something. If it isn't to the apparent, urgent things in your life, it is probably to the most fundamental, highly important things. Even when the urgent is good, the good can keep you from your best, keep you from your unique contribution, if you let it.
>
> —Stephen Covey

denigrate the importance of preaching, the return on training your laypeople can be tremendous. The value of having an army of workers versus doing ministry alone is enormous.

## Don't Let the Urgent Triumph Over the Important

Years ago, if someone sent you a letter and you responded within a week or so, it was acceptable. But today, with e-mail, text messaging, and voice mail, people expect an answer immediately, if not sooner. Such expectations give a sense of urgency to what may not even be important. Of course, some urgent communication is important, but much of it is not.

If you treat everything that comes across your desk or your computer screen as equally important, you will fail to give the truly important things the time they deserve. When you master sorting out the important from the urgent, you will come closer to Mark Victor Hansen's ideal: "Make your now wow, your minutes miracles, and your days pay. Your life will have been magnificently lived and invested, and when you die you will have made a difference."

## Exercise Courage

Courage might not be the first word that comes to mind when you think of organization, but it is a necessity. Tackling the more challenging, less pleasant tasks rather than putting them off requires courage. It also takes courage to decline invitations, offers, or demands that would delay or prevent you from accomplishing your priorities. Once you have established priorities and developed plans, exercise the courage necessary to follow through with them.

## Putting It Into Practice

Now that we've covered some key principles of organization, let's look at several best practices of solo pastors who achieve good organization in their lives and in their churches.

### Put Organizational Time on Your Calendar

Putting regular organizational time on your personal calendar can be a lifesaver. Take thirty minutes at the end of each week to plan for the upcoming week. What are your top priorities? What absolutely must be done next week? What else would you like to accomplish if you have additional time? List your goals and priorities so that you know exactly what you need to do and what you should do if you have time left over. This will give you a clear game plan for productivity in the upcoming week.

Then, at the end of each day, take fifteen minutes to plan the next day. Block out your time and assign yourself tasks from your priority list for each time frame. Be sure to allot a realistic amount of time—not too little and not too much. By spending a few minutes planning at the end of each day, you can walk into the office the next day with confidence, knowing what you need to accomplish and ready to hit the ground running.

### Build in Flex Time

In addition to blocking out time for specific tasks each day, be sure to build in flex time. There are almost always surprises and unexpected demands on the solo pastor's time. You may not be able to plan for all of it, but by blocking out thirty minutes or an hour of flex time each day (three to five hours each week),

---

*+≻— ≻≺+*

Have an open-door policy. That means anyone can talk to me, but I don't keep my door open. This way I'm not interrupted all the time. My staff and lay leaders know they can schedule a time to see me. I informally touch base with staff in the office halls and spend intentional time shooting the breeze a few minutes daily. This keeps me in touch with them while reserving a majority of my time focused on ministry tasks.

you'll be better prepared to respond to unanticipated needs without it adversely affecting your workflow. And if nothing comes up, you can use that time to get ahead in your sermon preparation!

When several needs or demands clamor for our attention, Alan Nelson suggests we go into triage mode. When an emergency room is flooded with patients, a triage nurse assigns priorities for treatment. You can do the same with the requests you receive on a daily basis. Such an approach looks at all the tasks with an eye toward what will yield the greatest benefit to the church and the people being served, and then places those items at the head of the line.[8]

## Develop Systems

A wise man once advised, "The first time you do something, do the best you can. The second time you do it, learn from the first time. The third time you do it, develop a system."

A system is a way of organizing your work so that you don't have to reinvent the wheel each time you want to ride a bike. Systems are your friend. To-do lists, calendars, libraries, computers, and strong positive habits are all servants of the organized pastor.

Many of the tasks of a solo pastor are done repeatedly. You regularly welcome newcomers, baptize people, receive new members, and train people for ministry. When you do tasks repeatedly, developing a system can help you handle those tasks more effectively and efficiently. For example, you may want to have a fellowship time for newcomers, followed by a membership preparation class, which would include a spiritual gifts inventory, two weeks later. This may be followed by a baptismal preparation class in another couple of weeks. All of these contacts may alert you to areas in which people need training, so you will want to schedule a training class for new teachers, or new ushers and greeters. Develop a system, so you know everything that needs to happen when you welcome newcomers.

Whatever you do, develop systems. They will help preserve your sanity as well as maximize your time and your contacts with people.

## Rounding Up the Strays

Cowboys and police eventually regained control of that cattle drive/parade in downtown Kansas City. They rounded up all the strays and herded them into a pen. Aside from one cowboy who broke his ankle when his horse slipped, no one else suffered an injury from the stampeding cattle.

You too can regain control of your life, your schedule, and your church, hopefully with a minimum of suffering, through good organizational practices.

> Learn how to separate the majors and the minors. A lot of people don't do well simply because they major in minor things.
>
> —Jim Rohn

Sir Edmund Hillary was a modest beekeeper in New Zealand until he gained worldwide fame by becoming the first man to scale Mount Everest. He said, "It is not the mountain we conquer, but ourselves." As we learn to discipline ourselves to organize our lives and our work, we will experience greater effectiveness personally and professionally.

## Action Steps for Becoming Organized

1. Determine the best time and place for you to have regular daily devotions. Start it and stick with it.
2. List three tasks you should stop doing immediately.
3. Schedule thirty minutes at the end of each week to plan your work for the next week. Schedule fifteen minutes at the end of each day to plan your work for the next day.
4. Choose someone you trust to hold you accountable for being better organized.
5. Determine two times during the day when you will check and respond to e-mails. Then discipline yourself to ignore e-mails the rest of the day.

# 2

# EQUIPPING
## Growing Spiritual Leaders

*You can be a leader of followers or a leader
of leaders; it's your choice.*

Pastor Phil is well on his way to becoming Super Pastor, which is not to be confused with becoming the pastor of a megachurch. Rather, a super pastor, as exemplified by Pastor Phil, is one who does it all.

He preaches the sermon on Sunday morning, chooses the music for the worship service, delivers the announcements, edits the bulletin, and occasionally even sings the special song. He also makes all the hospital calls, nursing home visits,

A leader is not a person who can do the work better than his followers; he is a person who can get his followers to do the work better than he can.

—Fred Smith

and shut-in contacts. He teaches a Bible study for adults on Wednesday evenings. He also chairs the monthly board meetings and attends every meeting of every committee. He conducts all the counseling sessions, whether for premarital, marriage, or crisis needs. Occasionally he provides transportation for parishioners who have doctors' appointments, and he often mows the church lawn. He is nearly omnipresent.

Pastor Phil doesn't want or try to be super pastor. He's not sure why or how it happened, and he definitely knows there's something wrong with this picture. But he doesn't really believe anything can be done about it. It must just go with the territory.

## Lone Rangership

Whether he knows it or not, Pastor Phil, like many other pastors, is not really engaged in leadership at all, but lone rangership. A leader guides a group of people to accomplish a common purpose; a lone ranger accomplishes everything himself while others watch.

### Making the Best Use of God's Precious Gifts

A pastor's calling is to equip other people so they can use their gifts to become partners in ministry, rather than just recipients of ministry.

When pastors exercise lone rangership rather than leadership, they prevent the church from receiving the full benefit of the gifts God has given his people. Rather than being actively involved in ministry, church members sit and watch as the pastor runs to and fro trying to accomplish everything that needs to happen. Not only does this limit the ministry of the church to what one person is able to accomplish, it also stunts the growth of God's people and of the kingdom itself.

On the other hand, when pastors fulfill their calling to equip the saints for ministry, they discover that:

- People have spiritual gifts they can use to make a difference in other people's lives for the Kingdom;
- When they use their gifts in ministry, people grow spiritually much more than what they would as passive recipients of ministry;
- People experience great joy and satisfaction because they are making a difference in others' lives;
- The pastor's own ministry is multiplied far beyond what could be accomplished alone;
- God receives the glory and his kingdom benefits in a tremendous way.

Added to all of that, when God's plan of equipping the saints is put into practice, the pastor is freed to live a more balanced, healthy life, and avoid some of the occupational hazards of a leadership position. Imagine that! Follow God's plan, solo pastor, and you can experience a healthier way of life.

## Avoiding Burnout and Brownout

Lone rangership can very easily lead to ministry fatigue and failure. Craig Brian Larson makes a distinction between burnout and brownout.[1] *Burnout* occurs when pastors drive themselves so relentlessly they flame out into a pile of ashes. *Brownout* occurs when pastors become so exhausted they no longer care, like the tennis player who becomes so tired after several sets that he loses the desire to win. The loneliness of

> Leadership is the capacity and will to rally men and women to a common purpose, and the character which inspires confidence.
>
> —Bernard L. Montgomery,

lone rangership can produce a debilitating weariness.

Christianity Today International conducted a research study about pastors' work weeks. About 20 percent of pastors reported working more than sixty-five hours a week. The average pastor spends 20 percent of that time on sermon preparation. Three-fourths of pastors would like to spend more time in prayer or sermon preparation. About 40 percent of pastors have expressed concern to a board member or other church leader about their workload. Slightly more than 20 percent of the pastors surveyed experienced termination or a forced resignation from a pastoral position.[2]

The problem is not necessarily that pastors work hard and put in long hours. Most people in executive leadership positions do. The problem arises when a pastor tries to do it all alone, rather than following God's plan of equipping the saints for ministry.

## Putting Away Insecurity

Solo pastors can save their sanity and their health by sharing their ministry with others. Unfortunately, I have known a few pastors who were too insecure to share ministry. Such pastors worry that someone else will get the credit, someone else will shine brighter than they do, and somehow they will be diminished in the eyes of the congregation. Just the opposite is true, of course, because a better team makes a better church and the people see the pastor as a better leader.

Fred A. Manske Jr., former vice president of FedEx, says, "The ultimate leader is one who is willing to develop people to the point that they eventually surpass him or her in knowledge and ability."[3] Only a secure pastor becomes such a leader.

The way to overcome insecurity about who gets the credit is to learn to focus entirely on the mission. The best leaders are those who are so fully invested in accomplishing the mission that they don't worry about who gets the credit or reward. For them, seeing the mission accomplished is reward enough in itself. This is the essence of servant leadership, and nowhere is it more appropriate than in the church.

Jim Zorn, former quarterback for the Seattle Seahawks, exemplified this kind of servant leadership when he lost his number-one quarterback position to Dave Krieg. Zorn said, "Football is a team sport, and if Dave Krieg can get more wins for this team than I can, then he should be the quarterback, and I will back him up. I will support him. I will watch every play and try to see things he can't see. I'll talk to him. We'll be friends. And I will support the coaches' decision to make him the quarterback."[4]

Solo ministry means you're working without other paid staff. It doesn't have to mean lone rangership. God has given all Christians spiritual gifts they can use in ministry. When they receive good training and a chance to use those gifts in meaningful ministry (rather than sitting through endless committee meetings), they are often thrilled for the opportunity.

The leaders who work most effectively, it seems to me, never say "I." They don't think "I." They think "we." They think "team." They understand their job to be making the team function. They accept the responsibility and don't sidestep, but "we" gets the credit.
—Peter F. Drucker

Jack Welch, former CEO of General Electric, wrote a statement in his book *Winning* that every solo pastor should take to heart: "Before you are a leader, success is all about growing yourself. When you become a leader, success is all about growing others."[5]

## Biblical Precedent for Leadership Development

In Scripture you can find several examples of leadership development. Moses mentored Joshua, Elijah modeled ministry for Elisha, and Jesus discipled the Twelve. Paul equipped leaders and advised Timothy and Titus to do the same in their respective ministries (2 Tim. 2:2; Titus 1:5).

### Paul Mentored Timothy

One of Paul's first instructions to Timothy gives him authority to "command certain men not to teach false doctrines any longer" (1 Tim. 1:3). "With the authority of God's Word behind him," comments Robert Black, "and the welfare of God's church before him, he must defend God's truth, even if that involves a confrontation with error."[6]

*Perseverance and Prayer.* Paul taught the importance of perseverance when he reminded Timothy not to shipwreck his faith, but to "fight the good fight, holding on to faith and a good conscience" (1 Tim. 1:18–19).

The apostle counseled Timothy on the vital role of prayer when he urged him to offer "requests, prayers, intercession and thanksgiving . . . for everyone—for kings and all those in authority, that we may live peaceful and quiet lives in all godliness and holiness" (1 Tim. 2:1–2).

*Character and Example.* Paul stressed the importance of character when he gave Timothy a list of qualifications for church leaders, whom he called overseers and deacons, and even added a word or two regarding their wives. By developing leaders of good character, Paul reminded him, "those who have served well gain an excellent standing and great assurance in their faith in Christ Jesus" (1 Tim. 3:13).

Paul urged Timothy to be a good example to others "in speech, in life, in love, in faith and in purity" (1 Tim. 4:12). He also encouraged him to devote himself "to the public reading of Scripture, to preaching and to teaching" (1 Tim. 4:13) and not to neglect his "gift, which was given [him] through a prophetic message when the body of elders laid their hands on [him]" (1 Tim. 4:14). He admonished him to watch his "life and doctrine closely" (1 Tim. 4:16).

Timothy not only read Paul's letters but watched Paul model these same values. As Paul reminded him, "You, however, know all about my teaching, my way of life, my purpose, faith, patience, love, endurance, persecutions, sufferings—what kinds of things happened to me in Antioch, Iconium and Lystra, the persecutions I endured" (2 Tim. 3:10–11). With Paul's encouragement, Timothy would model similar values to the people he led.

*Finishing Well.* Paul modeled for Timothy a life in which he had fought the good fight, finished the race, kept the faith, and looked forward to the crown of righteousness (2 Tim. 4:7–8).

## Paul Mentored Titus

In the same vein, Paul gave Titus a list of character qualities for the elders and overseers (Titus 1:6–9). He taught Titus to

⊹⟫━ ━⟨⊹

> The final test of a leader is that he leaves behind in other people the convictions and will to carry on.
>
> — Walter Lippman

rebuke the "many rebellious people, mere talkers and deceivers" on the island of Crete (Titus 1:13, 10). He advised Titus to "teach what is in accord with sound doctrine" (Titus 2:1). He urged him to remind people to "live self-controlled, upright and godly lives in this present age" (Titus 2:12). He counseled Titus to "avoid foolish controversies" and gave instructions on how to deal with divisive persons (Titus 3:9–10).

In all these ways and more, Paul modeled for, mentored, and motivated Timothy, Titus, and other young leaders to develop the qualities necessary for Christian living and leadership. Consequently, when Paul died, the church did not die. He left Timothy, Titus, Silas, Luke, and others to carry on the work after him.

## Benefits of Developing Spiritual Leaders

Sometimes pastors are reluctant to equip others because they think they will be perceived as the superior person reaching down to help the inferior person. Fortunately, it doesn't have to be this way at all. You can invite people as colleagues in Christ to join you on a journey to enhance and develop your leadership skills together. The fact that you are the one guiding the journey does not preclude you in any way from having the humility to say that you need to grow too. Pastors who lead others on this journey will reap many benefits for their congregations and themselves.

## You Help People Grow Spiritually

People who enter a leadership role inevitably find themselves stretched and challenged in such a way that they need to draw closer to God and rely on him more fully. By walking with people through their journey of leadership development, you are helping them to grow spiritually in brand-new ways.

Waylon Moore suggests a core curriculum for training leaders that would contain the following basics: consistency in daily devotions, Bible study, Scripture memory, and prayer. Then he recommends teaching attitude development, in which the prospective leader learns to believe and claim God's promises, use simple witnessing tools, discern God's guidance, be filled with the Spirit, and gain victory over sin. Learning how to nurture and disciple others and gain a vision for reaching the world would round out the curriculum.[7]

Moore also points out how Jesus himself worked with the disciples both publicly and privately. Publicly, he preached, healed, taught, and worked miracles as the disciples watched. Privately, they saw him interceding, witnessing, nurturing, and discipling.

Paul said, "Follow my example, as I follow the example of Christ" (1 Cor. 11:1). In the same way, many people are watching your public ministry. As you walk with Christ, people will see your example and follow. Pay attention to the model of the Christian life you're demonstrating.

It's the private mentoring, however, that will pay the biggest dividends. Pouring our lives into prospective leaders multiplies our ministry. As prospective leaders sense our passion and learn the values, principles, and practices by which we guide our lives and ministries, it deepens their walk with Christ and strengthens the church.

## You Empower Others to Reach People Where They Live

No pastor can reach everyone. But we can reach many more as we learn to lead through others.

All good leaders realize that they themselves can never accomplish all they dream of; others must carry out their vision. So they invest in others, encourage them, train them, and enable them to succeed. The best leaders realize that there's plenty of success to go around, so they help those around them reach for the stars.

Developing leaders is the pastor's primary method of extending the congregation's vision and mission, of building a work that lasts. Even though it might injure our egos to think about it, people rarely remember our sermons and Bible studies. But they do remember principles they put into practice as we work with them one-to-one or in small groups.

When we give people opportunities to live out the principles we teach where they live and work, the results are dynamic. Laypeople have contacts we don't have. They know people we have never met. They operate in circles where we don't have access. They can touch lives we may never be able to reach.

So, it makes sense to work with prospective leaders. Find out their spiritual gifts. Teach them how to use their gifts to maximum advantage. Give them information, insight, inspiration, and some new skills that will make them more effective. From leading ministry teams to serving in the community, from welcoming newcomers to calling on shut-ins, lay leaders who are equipped for ministry will multiply your impact immeasurably.

## You Raise the Bar for Leaders

When pastors train their people to lead, it raises the expectations for lay leaders—providing the pastor gives them opportunities to lead. Teaching others without giving them a chance to put it into practice will only bring frustration. But teaching along with fresh opportunities to serve will bring fruitfulness.

John R. Mott, who received the Nobel Peace Prize in 1946, insisted that leaders should multiply their lives by developing younger men. This included giving them "full play and adequate outlet for their powers." He insisted these young leaders should be given heavy burdens of responsibility. They should be encouraged to use their initiative and be given authority to make final decisions about certain things. When they did well, they should receive recognition and generous credit. "The principal thing is to trust them."[8]

People will usually rise to the level of our expectation. If we don't expect them to do well, they will seldom surprise us. If, on the other hand, we raise the bar and set the expectations high, they respond to the challenge.

> You have achieved excellence as a leader when people will follow you everywhere if only out of curiosity.
>
> —Colin Powell

## You Produce Longer Tenures for Pastors and People

When pastors develop teams to come alongside them in ministry, it not only strengthens the pastor, it bolsters the church's entire ministry. Lay leaders who become a vital part of the ministry find that they are more inclined to stick around since they have invested a lot in the ministry and the church has invested a lot in them. Pastors who develop lay leaders tend to stay longer in a parish because they receive support from those they've invested in and, because of that support, they avoid spiraling down into burnout or brownout.

Studies have shown that a pastor's most effective ministry comes in the sixth, seventh, and eighth years of tenure. Many pastors never get the chance to enjoy such effectiveness because they leave after two or three years. While some are tempted to start over somewhere else, coasting for a couple of years by reusing message series already preached in their current congregation, there are real disadvantages to doing so. For one thing, you rob yourself and your current congregation of the opportunity to experience the effectiveness that only comes with long-term ministry. Plus, you rob your new congregation of the fresh insight and relevant application that comes only from preparing new sermons. When you're coasting rather than challenging yourself, you'll grow little, if at all. And believe me, if you don't grow, your church will not grow.

> ⊶ ⊷
>
> Delegation is an art. Most pastors are afraid to delegate and thus find themselves on a ministry treadmill, hoping they don't get "voted off the island."

Staying longer and investing yourself in equipping lay leaders takes you to a level of ministry that is fulfilling because you're growing. When you get better, the church gets better. When you grow, the church grows.

## Putting It Into Practice

Pastor Phil might well ask, "If I'm up to my neck in activities now, how can I find time to train new leaders?" It's a valid question.

The answer is that at first, it might bring even more pressure, unless he can find a way to drop or delay something. But the extra pressure will be a case of short-term pain for long-term gain. The benefits of having trained leaders far outweighs the temporary stress of getting them trained.

Three ways to work on leadership development are through modeling, mentoring, and maturing.

## Reach Spiritual Leaders through Modeling

A denominational supervisor sat with the board of a local church to discuss their pastor's performance review prior to a vote on renewing his term with the church. Susan spoke up and said, "One of the things I appreciate about Pastor is that he never asks us to do something he is not willing to do himself."

Laypeople notice when pastors model the kind of behavior they teach. When they see their pastor demonstrating servant leadership, they are more likely to mirror that quality.

## Engage Spiritual Leaders through Mentoring

Bobb Biehl defines mentoring as "a lifelong relationship, in which a mentor helps a protégé reach her/his God-given potential."[9] Mentoring involves sharing growth principles, biblical knowledge, and life skills with those whom you want to develop. The question pastors often ask is "How do I choose the people I want to mentor?" It's another way of asking, "How do I spot a potential leader?" As a solo pastor vitally in need of help, consider these ideas.

*Look for Persons of Character.* When the apostles chose deacons to oversee the distribution of food to widows, they first looked for men who were "well respected" (Acts 6:3 NLT). To accomplish this task, they had to be individuals whom others trusted and respected. Fred Smith says, "When leaders fail, more often it is a result of a character flaw than lack of competence."

*Select People with a Good Track Record.* The best predictor of future behavior is past behavior. People who are leaders in business, on the job, or in the neighborhood may also excel at leadership in the church. Not that business success automatically translates to success in spiritual leadership. A person must have the spiritual qualifications as well. But most often, a disciple of Jesus who leads well in business also has the capability of leading well in the church.

*Find People Who Inspire Others.* People who can spread excitement and enthusiasm to others are people worth mentoring for the cause of Christ. A positive mental attitude and an optimistic outlook on life are indispensable qualities for people who lead.

*Choose People Who Are Willing to Accept Responsibility.* It's easy to find people who want to climb the pay scale but don't want to accept the responsibility that goes with it. Those who are willing to take responsibility for a project are those who are likely to have excellent leadership skills.

*Look for People with Potential.* Before you make them chair of the task force, give them a place at the table. See how they do at helping to solve a problem before you entrust them with the whole responsibility. Dale Carnegie said, "I know men in the ranks who will not stay in the ranks. Why? Because they have the ability to get things done." When you find that kind of potential, you know you want that person on your team.

*Give Priority to People Who Have a Thick Skin.* Leaders often attract criticism. Small-minded people like to whittle others down to their size. If a prospective leader wilts under this kind of heat, it hurts his or her chances of success. Part of your mentoring will be to help young leaders put criticism in perspective and learn not to let it sink in too deeply.

*Select People Who Respect Others.* People who do not demonstrate deep respect for others will not be effective leaders. On the other hand, people who go out of their way to show respect for others are generally more likely to receive respect in return.

*Find People Who Have Their Family Life Together.* Does your potential leader have the respect of his or her family? After all, family members know us better than anyone else. They see us when our guard is down. So if they respect us, it says a great deal about character and personal values. Paul told Timothy that one qualification for potential church leaders is that they manage their own family well and their children respectfully follow their guidance (1 Tim. 3:4).

*Select People Who Don't Require Motivation.* In order to be an effective leader, a person must believe deeply in the mission and values of the congregation so that he or she is self-motivated. If you find yourself having to beg, plead, or otherwise cajole a person to join you in leadership development, you may not have the right person. Some people are reluctant because they lack confidence,

As for the best leaders, the people do not notice their existence. The next best, the people honor and praise. The next, the people fear; and the next, the people hate. When the best leader's work is done, the people say, "We did it ourselves."

—Lao-Tzu

and that's okay. You can build confidence. However, you can't instill motivation in another person. It comes from within.

## Develop Spiritual Leaders through Maturing

John D. Pinter, a pilot for United Airlines, recalls a little boy who came up to the cockpit after the plane landed. Pinter and his partners showed the boy all the bells and whistles. The lad said, "When I grow up, I want to be a pilot."

Pinter replied, only half-joking, "You can't do both, son."

I hope you have a childlike sense of wonder that God would use any of us in spiritual leadership, but we do have to grow up. When the pastor develops spiritual leaders, the pastor grows, the leaders grow, and it results in a more mature congregation. People learn to put pettiness aside. They learn to major on majors instead of majoring on minors. They learn to develop better priorities. They learn to pray more effectively, witness more confidently, and lead more humbly. Good leadership develops mature disciples.

## Saving Pastor Phil

It's been a year since Pastor Phil made a commitment to equip lay leaders to come alongside him in ministry, and today it's a different picture. Instead of feeling like a solo pastor, he feels like a team leader. No longer does he attend every committee meeting. Instead he communicates regularly with committee chairpersons and trusts them to lead the committees. Shut-ins are receiving a lot more visits, because he's no longer the only one visiting. Trained lay leaders are now sharing that responsibility. Frankly, they're better at it than he is. Lay leaders are helping with hospital visitation and preparing the bulletin. Pastor Phil's wife sees much more of her husband now, and she's thrilled that he's not as stressed-out as he was. While equipping people does require some effort, Phil has decided it's more than worth the time and energy, and he plans to continue to make it a high priority in his future ministry.

## Action Steps for Developing Leaders

1. Using the guidelines for selecting potential leaders, make a list of those who would be best suited for a leadership role in your church.
2. Select two or three prospective leaders with whom you can begin meeting regularly to provide mentoring for them.
3. Find a spiritual gifts inventory you can begin to use with potential leaders.
4. Make a list of all the tasks you do regularly and determine to whom you can delegate some things.
5. Begin to delegate, making sure you are clear in your guidelines and expectations. Remember to follow up and provide accountability for their performance.

# 3

# PASTORAL CARE
## Developing an
## Intensive Caring Ministry

*The word* pastor *implies one who cares for others.*

Who do you suppose holds the world record for the number of funerals conducted in one year? My vote would go to Martin Rinkert, a pastor in Eilenburg, Germany, in the first half of the seventeenth century. It was a tumultuous time; the Thirty Years' War began in 1618 and continued until the Peace of Westphalia in 1648. Thousands of people died during the war, and this small town was caught in the middle of it. In one year alone, Pastor Rinkert conducted funerals for more than five thousand people, an average of more than fourteen per day!

I'm not just a professional; I'm an extension of the love of Christ, a channel of his grace.

—Robert J. Morgan

Yet amid all that misery, Pastor Rinkert composed a table grace that eventually became a great hymn of thanksgiving:

Now thank we all our God
With hearts and hands and voices,
Who wondrous things has done,
In whom this world rejoices.

A spirit that can find gratitude in such times must truly understand God's heart for pastoral care. Likely neither you nor I will ever be called upon to render service of that magnitude. Yet you may be called to give pastoral care in unique circumstances, such as a pastor friend recently shared with me.

> Be sensitive to the plight of others. You have to know about the tragedies as well as the triumphs, the failures as well as the successes.
>
> —Jim Rohn

The bride and groom had just left the church, the custodian was sweeping up the rice, and the wedding reception would not start for another hour. The pastor decided to stop by the hospital to visit a parishioner whose brother had been involved in a serious motorcycle accident and was hanging on to life by a thread.

As he entered the intensive care waiting room, facial expressions around the room told him all he needed to know. Their loved one had just died in surgery. The pastor cared for and prayed with the family, asking God to give them grace and peace in their time of terrible sorrow and loss. He promised to check in again with them later.

Then, after some tearful embraces, he drove straight to the wedding reception, arriving in time to offer a celebratory prayer before the meal. In the space of less than thirty minutes, he lived Paul's instructions: "Rejoice with those who rejoice; mourn with those who mourn" (Rom. 12:15).

For a solo pastor, there is no question about whether to be involved in pastoral care. You are thrust into it, whether you like it or not, whether you are ready or not. The only question is "How can I and the congregation provide the most effective care?"

## The Challenges of Pastoral Care

Providing effective pastoral care can be difficult for a number of reasons. Few pastors feel they received adequate training in school to minister effectively to people one-to-one. Beyond issues of equipping there are other challenges as well.

### Pulpit Ministry versus One-to-one Ministry

Many a pastor, quite at home in the pulpit, is anxious at the prospect of connecting with people one-to-one, whether to offer compassion in a time of loss or to offer support and counsel in the middle of a crisis. One novice pastor, upon hearing that a parishioner was diagnosed with an advanced stage of breast cancer, delayed visiting her at the hospital. When asked why he didn't come sooner, he said, "Seminary did not prepare me for this."

J. H. Jowett, in one of his Yale lectures, said,

> The difficulty of delivering a message is in inverse proportion to the size of the audience. To face the individual soul with the Word of God . . . is one of the heaviest commissions given to our church. Where there are ten men who can face a crowd, there is only one who can face the individual. Gentleman, it seemed as

though I could preach a sermon and never meet a devil. But as soon as I began to take my sermon to the individual, the streets were thick with devils.[1]

Most of us do not literally preach our sermons to individuals, but we do give messages of care, comfort, and counsel to individuals on a regular basis. The good news is that, despite how you might feel right now, you can learn to deliver such messages in a way that offers hope and encouragement.

## People Have Different Expectations

Another challenge with pastoral care is that individuals' desires and expectations can vary so widely. On the one hand, pastors encounter people who say they'd rather not be bothered by the pastor one-to-one. They come to church for the preaching, but prefer to remain more or less anonymous.

On the other hand, pastors encounter parishioners who seem never to get enough pastoral care. They schedule regular counseling appointments and rehearse the same problems or maladies in session after session. They often counter your attempts to provide support or counsel with "I've done all that stuff before and it didn't help." Such people don't want to get better; they want attention.

Between such extremes are the vast majority of people who don't want to be a nuisance but do appreciate pastoral care when they are going through difficulties. In fact, just knowing that the pastor and congregation cares is a tremendous encouragement to them.

### The Countless Multitudes

Another pastoral care challenge, especially for the solo pastor, is the sheer number of people in the congregation or community who demand time from the pastor. It can be quite overwhelming for a pastor to look out at the congregation and see all the people needing care in the upcoming week and to wonder how to fit it all in.

As a solo pastor, I want you to know you're not alone in your struggle to balance the demands of pastoral care with all the other important ministry functions of your job. I also want to encourage you: There are ways to lighten the pastoral care load you're currently bearing, while still providing excellent care for your people.

As I said in another place, "There will never be a substitute for your personal care of those in your congregation or organization. People need *you*. There will be times when they need you 'in person.' They will need your prayers. They will need that shared promise from God's Word."[2] At the same time, the burden for pastoral care ministry doesn't have to fall on the shoulders of the pastor alone. More about that after we look at some of what the Bible has to say about pastoral care.

## The Biblical Concept of Shepherding

Perhaps the most powerful metaphor for pastoral care in Scripture is that of a shepherd tending sheep. It's interesting to note that, in the Bible, a variety of individuals fulfill the role of shepherd for God's people.

## God Is Our Shepherd

The Bible is replete with references to God as our shepherd. David's famous statement, "The LORD is my shepherd," leaps to mind immediately. Yet it was Jacob, with hands outstretched in blessing on the heads of Joseph's sons, Ephraim and Manasseh, who first referred to God as his shepherd: "May the God before whom my fathers Abraham and Isaac walked, the God who has been my shepherd all my life to this day, the Angel who has delivered me from all harm—may he bless these boys" (Gen. 48:15–16).

When Moses sought a successor, he prayed, "May the LORD, the God of the spirits of all mankind, appoint a man over this community to go out and come in before them, one who will lead them out and bring them in, so the LORD's people will not be like sheep without a shepherd" (Num. 27:16–17).

Jesus referred to himself as the Good Shepherd (John 10:11), and Peter called him the Chief Shepherd (1 Pet. 5:4). Jesus, our greatest example of pastoral care, saw the people through compassionate eyes and healed them of "every disease and sickness. When he saw the crowds, he had compassion on them, because they were harassed and helpless, like sheep without a shepherd" (Matt. 9:35–36). Roger L. Hahn contends that Jesus' compassion was not directed only at their physical suffering. "Rather, it was the disruption of their lives and the loss of God's peace that moved Jesus. . . . His ministry was not just to heal but to restore hope."[3]

## Pastors Are Called to be Shepherds

But God is not the only shepherd of his people. He also empowers the leaders of his people to provide for their needs.

Ezekiel the prophet described the leaders of Israel as shepherds, even as he took them to task for failing to fulfill their responsibility. He prophesied against the leaders of Israel, saying, "Woe to the shepherds of Israel who only take care of themselves! Should not shepherds take care of the flock? . . . So they were scattered because there was no shepherd" (Ezek. 34:2, 5).

> The pastoral office is by definition a shepherding task. . . . Shepherding cannot be done at a sterile distance, with automated telephone answering services, computerized messages, and impersonal form letters. By definition there cannot be an absentee shepherd. There can be no mail-order or mechanized pastoral service, because pastoring is personal. It is not just public talk but interpersonal meeting where richer self-disclosures are possible.
>
> —Thomas C. Oden

Later, as Paul was helping to organize the young church, he told the elders of the church at Ephesus, "Keep watch over yourselves and all the flock of which the Holy Spirit has made you overseers. Be shepherds of the church of God, which he bought with his own blood. I know that after I leave, savage wolves will come in among you and will not spare the flock" (Acts 20:28–29).

Peter used similar words to instruct the elders among his readers: "Be shepherds of God's flock that is under your care, serving as overseers—not because you must, but because you are willing, as God wants you to be; not greedy for money, but eager to serve; not lording it over those entrusted to you, but being examples to the flock. And when the Chief Shepherd appears, you will receive the crown of glory that will never fade away" (1 Pet. 5:2–4).

## Laypersons Can Be Effective Shepherds

Shepherding, though, is not limited in Scripture to professional pastors. All God's people are expected to shepherd one another. In Galatians 6:2, Paul instructed Christians to "carry each other's burdens, and in this way you

> Those who bring sunshine to the lives of others cannot keep it from themselves.
>
> —James M. Barrie

will fulfill the law of Christ." He also instructed pastors to equip laypeople to minister to one another: "It was he who gave some to be . . . pastors and teachers . . . to prepare God's people for works of service, so that the body of Christ may be built up" (Eph. 4:11–12).

# Caregiving—It's Essential

A recent Gallup survey asked people why they were satisfied or not satisfied with the churches they attend. Eighty-four percent of those who claim to be "very satisfied" with their churches report that "the spiritual leaders of my congregation seem to care for me as a person." Of those who were "somewhat satisfied" with their churches, only 36 percent believe their leaders care about them. Among those who claim to be "very satisfied" with their churches, almost 90 percent say "the spiritual leaders of my congregation seem to care for each other."[4]

The same survey indicated that church members value "personal interaction with the pastor or minister." Eighty-four percent of members say their pastor knows them by name. We may debate about whether such feelings and expectations are good and right, but the fact remains that most Christians expect their pastors to be available and deeply interested in their lives, particularly when they are hurting. Here are some principles that can help the solo pastor develop an effective ministry of pastoral care.

### There Is No Substitute for Spending Time with People

Some pastors are office oriented; others are people oriented. Those who like to spend time in the office will have to discipline themselves to spend time with people, and vice versa. Whether you are the former or the latter or a happy mixture of both, your ministry will be stronger when you spend a reasonable amount of time with people.

When Richard Halverson, former chaplain of the United States Senate, was a pastor, he would schedule a breakfast or lunch, particularly with leaders in his church. He would discuss their jobs, their families, their hobbies, and anything that interested them. Often someone would ask what his agenda was in meeting with them.

Dr. Halverson would say, "I just wanted to spend some time with you." That simple act spoke volumes about the pastor's care for them.

### Everyone Wants to Be Accepted

People ask themselves three questions when they visit a new church. "Will I fit in?" "Will I be able to find a friend?" "Will there be anything for me to do?" It's all part of our desire to be accepted and our need for relationships.

Dr. James Lynch says adults without deep relationships have a death rate twice as high as those who regularly interact with others. In our culture, many people watch their calories and check their cholesterol religiously, but ignore the development of their relationships. Our relational life has as big an impact on physical health as obesity, smoking, high blood pressure, and lack of exercise.[5]

God created us to enjoy relationships. That's why so many people eagerly seek friendship online or through other means. The church is a place where people can find connectivity. Good pastoral care brings people together. As people develop friendships and healthy connections, they will do a great deal of pastoral care for themselves.

It was after Dwight L. Moody heard Henry Moorehouse speak on John 3:16 for a week that he began to comprehend the life-changing power of God's love. Moody said, "This heart of mine began to thaw out; I could not keep back the tears. I just drank it in. . . . I tell you there is one thing that draws about everything else in the world, and that is love." He added, "The churches would soon be filled if outsiders could find that people in them loved them when they came. This . . . draws sinners! We must win them to us first, then we can win them to Christ."

## People Are Loyal to the Congregation That Cares for Them

Some people will, of course, be loyal to a local congregation simply because they feel called by God to participate in its ministry. Most people, however, develop loyalty to a faith community because of the relationships they've developed there. They need to feel cared for and loved before they are ready to jump in to participate and serve. Not that your congregation will attach strings to the care you provide. Our congregations' service and ministry should always be a free gift out of the abundance of mercy and grace God has offered each of us. But, as a byproduct of such ministry, people often feel a sense of connection and loyalty because they received care. This is a normal and healthy response of gratitude. Your congregation will greatly benefit from such loyalty as you provide excellent care for people who are hurting.

## Christians Can Uniquely Minister to the Whole Person

Christians are in a position to minister to people's physical, spiritual, and emotional needs. No other organization can touch people on all fronts as well as the church can. But meeting needs in this way requires the church to function at a high level.

When people are physically ill, we pray for them. When they are spiritually distressed, when they need Christ, when they are facing heavy temptations, we pray for them. We encourage and support them. We can lead them to Christ, to Scripture, and to spiritual wholeness. When they are emotionally distraught, we offer hope. As Corrie Ten Boom said, "No pit is so deep but God is deeper still."

> God did not write solo parts for us. He has divine connections for you—the right friends and the right associations.
>
> —John Mason

Robert J. Morgan suggests several reasons pastors are uniquely positioned to give superior care.

*Pastors Care as Friends.* When people come to us with their problems, they approach someone who cares for them. We may not have all the answers, but we can love, listen, and pray.

*Pastors Build on Existing Relationships.* When parishioners seek our help, they are coming to a person with whom they have worshiped every week, with whom they have met in boards and committees, whom they have seen visiting in the hospital, baptizing their children, conducting funerals and weddings. The connections are already there.

*Pastors Preach Care every Sunday.* As the apostle Paul told the Ephesian elders, "You know that I have not hesitated to preach anything that would be helpful to you but have taught you publicly and from house to house" (Acts 20:20).

*Pastors Give Biblical Solutions for Spiritual Issues.* As Morgan says, "There is no better tool than Scripture for penetrating soul and spirit, joints and marrow, thoughts and intents."[6]

## Laypersons Make Excellent Caregivers

As a solo pastor's ministry grows, it will soon become too large for him to care for all alone. Yet the church may not be able to afford additional staff. Training laypersons to be caregivers will add immeasurably to a local church's effectiveness.

Inviting laypeople to serve as caregivers is also an excellent way to involve people in ministry who may never feel comfortable or capable singing, preaching, or praying in public. Yet they can use their gifts of compassion and mercy to make a significant difference in another person's life.

# The Practice of Caregiving

A pastor has twenty-four hours in a day, just like everyone else. Yet the expectations to be there for others and to know what to say and do are high. How can you excel at this important aspect of ministry?

## Ninety-Minutes-a-Day Care

I have often recommended a simple method for ministering to several individuals in your congregation each day.

*Spend One Hour in One-to-One Ministry.* You can meet in your office if that works for the person you're caring for. But I have found it most effective to meet people at a restaurant for lunch, breakfast, or coffee. I always pick up the tab. (If your church does not have a budget line item for such ministry opportunities, it would be good to suggest one at your next finance committee meeting.) Your agenda for such meetings is simply to listen to the other person and understand the thoughts and concerns of his or her heart, providing support and encouragement as you can. Naturally, if you meet someone of the opposite sex, be sure their spouse or your spouse is present.

How far you go in life depends on you being tender with the young, compassionate with the aged, sympathetic with the striving, and tolerant of the weak and the strong. Because someday in life you will have been all of these.

—George Washington Carver

*Spend Fifteen Minutes on Correspondence.* In that short period of time, you can write three brief notes, e-mails, or text messages to people in your congregation. You can use this time to remember people's birthdays or anniversaries. Be sure your church logo is printed on the card (in case your handwriting is as bad as mine) so they'll know who sent it! Make the notes sincere, short, specific, and spontaneous.

*Spend Fifteen Minutes on Phone Calls.* Again, you can use this method to remember parishioners' birthdays or anniversaries, or simply to cover your membership list systematically.

Let people know you are thinking about them, ask if there is anything they would like you to be praying about, and wish them a great day.

In just ninety minutes a day, you can accomplish a great deal of personal contact with your church family that sends a clear message of love and concern for them.

## Does Anyone Make House Calls Anymore?

In some communities, a pastor does not dare to drop in uninvited. It is always best to make appointments. In other communities, especially rural areas, people are almost offended if you don't drop in unannounced. Some members would rather not see you unless there's a problem. Others will wonder why you don't ever call on them.

In order to learn your congregation's desires and expectations, try this procedure. Announce to your people that you would love to sit down with them in their homes and get better acquainted. However, you don't know their schedules and when it would be a good time to visit. Would they do you a favor by extending an invitation when it fits their schedule?

When people call, you can set up a mutually agreeable time to visit in their home. If some wonder why you haven't contacted them, remind them of your invitation and encourage them to give you a call at any time.

## Use Contact Cards

A contact card in the weekly worship folder gives people an opportunity to share their prayer requests, special needs, upcoming surgeries, or requests for an appointment. If you use the cards consistently, your people will grow accustomed to communicating with you in this way.

When you receive information from contact cards, be sure to follow up right away. If you don't, people will think this method of communication is ineffective—or worse, that you don't really care.

## Differentiate Between a Crisis and a Problem

Not every problem requires a pastor to drop everything and run to a parishioner's rescue. Even something that seems to be a crisis may not be urgent upon careful investigation.

A member called one Saturday afternoon as the pastor was putting the finishing touches on his sermon. This member told Pastor she needed to see him right away because her marriage was falling apart. He asked, "How long has this been going on?"

"Oh, for years," she replied.

He candidly said, "You know, right now I'm in the middle of finishing my sermon, and honestly, I wouldn't be at my best. Since it's been going on for a long time anyway, if you think you could wait until Monday, I could more easily give you my undivided attention."

She was agreeable and they scheduled a time two days later when she came to the office. That approach might not work with everyone, so a pastor needs to be sensitive. Yet defining boundaries, along with determining whether it's a crisis or a chronic problem, may help the minister be more effective.

## Be a Good Listener

When it comes to providing pastoral care, avoid the temptation to try to kill two birds with one stone. Pastors have many things on their minds: the sermon needs work, hospital calls are waiting, an outline for a newsletter article is forming vaguely in the brain. Turning off those competing interests is absolutely essential for focused listening. Listening with focused intent will help you be a better listener, and people who are hurting need your undivided attention.

Body language is also important. Looking directly at the person, leaning forward, asking clarifying questions, and maintaining a body posture that says "I'm listening" all communicate to the speaker that you are paying attention. The net result is that you will understand your friend better and you can offer more effective care.

## Cast a Vision for a Caring Church

Resources—money, time, and personnel—are limited in a solo ministry. If a pastor can inspire and train the congregation to become more caring, they can provide valuable pastoral care for one another. When you or others tell stories about how the members of your congregation are effectively caring for and ministering to one another, it helps people to know they are not alone. When they're hurting, God's people will provide support and care.

If you're looking for a way to take caregiving to the next level at your congregation, Stephen Ministries

Leaders have to keep lifting up the vision of a place where everyone feels at home and help develop structures where that can happen. It might be on a ministry team. It might be in geographically based "home groups." It might be through intergenerational Sunday school classes, or some other creative approach. But if we don't push our passion for a church where no one is left out, it won't happen.

—Larry and Annie Mercer

(www.stephenministries.org) offers a number of resources, as well as a comprehensive system for training laypeople to provide excellent care.

### Develop a Team to Do "At-the-Door" Calling

When you follow up with new people in your community, it might be good to call ahead. But whether your laypeople drop by or make an appointment, be sure your guests understand it will only be an at-the-door visit. No one will enter their home. Maybe your laypersons will leave a bag of cookies or a loaf of homemade bread, along with a newcomers' packet from the church. They might also ask if the church can pray for any special needs, then communicate those needs back to the church so they can be lifted up in intercessory prayer. Such at-the-door calling can be an effective way to touch people with a minimum of intrusion.

### Double Your Team of Caregivers

Tony Morgan and Tim Stevens recommend developing a community where "shoulder-tapping" becomes the responsibility of the laypeople.[7] When you need new volunteers, encourage your current volunteers to invite people with whom they already have relationships to join them in serving. If each caregiver taps the shoulder of another person who is not currently serving, you will double your team within one year.

## Becoming an Intentional Caregiver

You can enhance your care-giving by being alert and intentional about caring, even in ordinary situations. A little girl came up to her pastor in the church foyer following the worship service. Without saying a word, she lifted a finger that was tightly wrapped with an adhesive bandage. The pastor, without saying a word, unwrapped the bandage, kissed the girl's finger, and wrapped it back up again. That small act communicated volumes of pastoral care.

Another pastor made telephone calls to people who had been absent from church more than one Sunday. This can be tricky, because people resent it if they think you are checking up on them. He would simply say, "Hello, this is Pastor, and I just called to tell you I missed you last Sunday."

If they offered some excuse or explanation, he typically would not comment, unless they had been ill or suffered some crisis. Instead, he would remind them, "Well, I just wanted you to know I missed you." During the course of a short conversation, no more than two or three minutes, he would remind them more than once that he missed them.

When they put down the telephone and someone said, "Who was that?" they would answer, "It was Pastor."

"What did he want?"

"He wanted me to know he missed me."

What a great message to leave with people! It speaks volumes about pastoral care.

## Action Steps for Developing a Pastoral Care Ministry

1. Make a list of people you can spend an hour with this week as a part of your new ninety-minutes-a-day plan.

2. Determine the top three to five people in your congregation who would make excellent care-givers. Begin making plans to invite them to be trained for care-giving ministry.

3. Start a file folder of stories about laypersons who excel at care-giving. Be sure to respect people's privacy by asking their permission before sharing a story.

4. Evaluate your church's approach to newcomers. What does it say about your congregation's concern for others?

# 4

# PROCLAMATION
## The Power of Positive Preaching

*The most visible thing pastors do is preach.*

You should have heard Charles Stanley's sermon on television this morning, Pastor. It was awesome!" Fred exuded as he pumped the pastor's hand after the service.

Pastor Jim muttered to himself, "When your wife was in the hospital, why didn't you call *him* to come and visit her?" But audibly he said, "God bless you, Fred. Sounds like you've had a great morning!"

Pastor Jim's sermon was actually quite good. It was biblical, well illustrated, and spoke to the

Great sermons take place when flint strikes steel. When the flint of a person's problem strikes the steel of the Word of God, you get a spark, and the spark will burn.

—Haddon Robinson

congregation's needs. Most people received it well and felt it was helpful. But Fred's exuberant comments about the television preacher stuck with Pastor Jim all day, like an undigested piece of beef. *How in the world am I supposed to compete with these superstars?*

## The Challenge of Preaching

Preaching is the most visible thing pastors do. When congregations search for a new pastor, one of the first questions they ask is "Can he preach?" It's also the part of the pastor's ministry that people are most likely to criticize.

+>═══• •═══<+

God makes his ministers a flame of fire. Am I ignitable? God, deliver me from the dread asbestos of "other things." Saturate me with the oil of thy Spirit that I may be a flame. Make me thy fuel, Flame of God.

—Jim Elliot

The Institute for Advanced Pastoral Studies took a survey and asked churchgoers, "What do you think of sermons?" Some sample responses:

"Too much analysis and too little answer."

"Too impersonal, too propositional—they relate nothing to life."

"Most sermons resemble hovercrafts skimming over the water on blasts of hot air, never landing anyplace!"

Someone sarcastically defined a sermon as "the fine art of talking in someone else's sleep."[1]

The effectiveness of preaching, though, cannot be judged based on the number of positive or negative comments you hear at the end of a service. The only measure that matters is changed lives. A number of factors make preaching for life-change a challenge in today's environment.

## Connecting

Most people decide within the first two or three sentences of a sermon whether it will be worth their effort to pay attention. What makes a sermon worth the effort? It must contain information people perceive as relevant to their lives. If you don't make an immediate connection with your listeners, you'll find yourself fighting an uphill battle to regain their attention.

## Holding Interest

Maintaining interest in a sermon has perhaps never been more difficult than in today's over stimulated, short-attention-span world. Yet the Scriptures we preach are the message of life. It is the preacher's task to speak God's living Word in such a way that listeners experience its vitality. Through God's Spirit and your hard work, you can do just that. You don't have to be a scintillating orator to keep your congregation's interest. But it does require thorough preparation and attentiveness to the principles of effective communication.

I'd like to challenge the notion that people are less interested in preaching than two thousand years ago. People are as interested as ever in finding meaning for their lives. In fact, one could argue that Americans are eagerly grubbing around for meaning. . . . People are busy listening for something.

—William Willimon

## Behaving Humbly

There is a fine line to walk between speaking God's Word with authority and speaking it with arrogant self-importance. Pastors should resist the temptation to present themselves as larger than life, or more godly or spiritual than others in the congregation. When speaking from the pulpit each Sunday, it can be a challenge to maintain an appropriate attitude of humility, and to remember that we are finite, fallen human beings too. We do well to remember the words of the apostle Paul when he said, "Who is equal to such a task?" (2 Cor. 2:16).

To gifted preachers, Martyn Lloyd-Jones gave this warning: "Watch your natural gifts. . . . Watch your strength, not so much weakness. It is your strength you have to watch, the things at which you excel, your natural gifts and aptitudes. They are the ones most likely to trip you because they are the ones that will tempt you to make a display or to pander to self. So watch these and also your idiosyncrasies."[2]

## Encouraging People

It is all too easy for a pastor to look out at a congregation and see nothing but their flaws. We can forget that ours is a message of grace and hope, rather than condemnation, even for those who have failed for what seems like the thousandth time. Sometimes, rather than encouraging, we want to blast people instead. While it's true that we are called both to comfort the afflicted and afflict the comfortable, we ought always to hold out hope and to offer encouragement.

## Respecting People

It is easy to become sarcastic if you feel you are talking in a vacuum, if you are getting no feedback, or wondering whether your preaching makes a difference. But we make a mistake when we inject bitter sarcasm into our sermons. Sarcasm shows a lack of respect and is more likely to injure and divide than to heal and unify. Always take the high road. Never take out your frustrations on the congregation. Be mature enough to deal with problems one-to-one instead of lashing out from the pulpit.

## Coaching People

A large part of preaching is helping people see where they are falling short and how they can do better through the power of the Holy Spirit. It is a challenge to confront people with their deficiencies without coming across as being critical. Rather than criticizing, think of your ministry of correction as coaching and helping people become the best they can be. This doesn't mean you avoid talking about issues. In fact, you confront them directly. But you do so with a spirit of cooperation rather than antagonism.

> God help the preacher who abandons his ideals! But at the same time, God pity the preacher who is so idealistic he fails to be realistic. A realist is an idealist who has gone through the fire and been purified. A skeptic is an idealist who has gone through the fire and been burned. There is a difference.
>
> —Warren Wiersbe

# Biblical Preaching

Biblical preaching has been a central focus since the days of the early church. Peter gave the first sermon of the Christian era on the day of Pentecost. His message and the events that occurred that day produced several responses from the people in Jerusalem.

## Preaching Evokes a Response

"Amazed and perplexed, they asked one another, 'What does this mean?' Some, however, made fun of them and said, 'They have had too much wine.' . . . When the people heard this, they were cut to the heart and said to Peter and the other apostles, 'Brothers, what shall we do?' . . . Those who accepted his message were baptized, and about three thousand were added to their number that day" (Acts 2:12–13, 37, 41). Note the responses:

- Some were amazed.
- Some were perplexed.
- Some made fun (mocked).
- Some were cut to the heart.
- Some believed.

Preaching continues to elicit similar reactions to this day.

### God Uses the "Foolishness of Preaching"

Paul said, "For since in the wisdom of God the world through its wisdom did not know him, God was pleased through the foolishness of what was preached to save those who believe" (1 Cor. 1:21).

Not that Paul really thought preaching is foolish. He was speaking from the world's perspective. But God takes pleasure in using what people consider foolishness to transform hearts and lives. Of course, no one wants to have their work described as foolishness, but it all depends on what audience you're hoping to please. Paul went on to say that what some consider foolishness is actually the wisdom of God:

"Jews demand miraculous signs and Greeks look for wisdom, but we preach Christ crucified: a stumbling block to Jews and foolishness to Gentiles, but to those whom God has called, both Jews and Greeks, Christ the power of God and the wisdom of

God. For the foolishness of God is wiser than man's wisdom, and the weakness of God is stronger than man's strength" (1 Cor. 1:22–25).

## Preaching is Effective

It is easy to believe in the effectiveness of a great evangelist's preaching or in the preaching of a well-known megachurch pastor, but it might not be so easy to believe in the effectiveness of your own preaching. But God has promised to bless his Word wherever it is uttered, even by preachers who are unknown to the masses, laboring in out-of-the-way places. Here's why:

"As the rain and the snow come down from heaven, and do not return to it without watering the earth and making it bud and flourish, so that it yields seed for the sower and bread for the eater, so is my word that goes out from my mouth: It will not return to me empty, but will accomplish what I desire and achieve the purpose for which I sent it" (Isa. 55:10–11).

However, preaching can only hope to be effective when it is biblical preaching, where the primary focus and result is to hear and apply God's Word.

As the preacher climbs the steps to the pulpit with his sermon in hand, he hikes his black robe over his knees so he will not trip over it on the way up. His mouth is a little dry. He has cut himself shaving. He feels as if he has swallowed an anchor. . . .

The stakes have never been higher. Two minutes from now the preacher may have lost his listeners completely to their own thoughts, but at this moment, the silence is deafening. Everyone knows the kinds of things he has told them before, but who knows what this time, out of the silence, he will tell them?

—Frederick Buechner

69

## Preaching Equips People for God's Work

Paul wrote to Timothy, "All Scripture is God-breathed and is useful for teaching, rebuking, correcting and training in righteousness, so that the man of God may be thoroughly equipped for every good work" (2 Tim. 3:16–17).

Paul named four things the Scriptures can accomplish. When our sermons are based on Scripture, they can accomplish these things too.

*Teaching—the Knowledge of Scripture.* Preach through a book of the Bible sometime and see if it doesn't increase both your understanding of the Word as well as the congregation's.

*Rebuking—the Violation of Scripture.* When people in your congregation are violating the clear teaching of Scripture, the Word of God is the most effective means of addressing the issue.

*Correcting—the Misunderstanding of Scripture.* The Greek word Paul used in 2 Timothy 3:16 for correction means "straightening up." The image is of people whose lives are crooked because of warped teaching or philosophy. Part of the pastor's responsibility in preaching is to correct people's beliefs so they can walk upright again.

*Training—in Application of Scripture.* The goal of preaching is that people's lives would be changed. This can only happen when your people are able to see how Scripture applies to their lives.

The goal of all teaching, rebuking, correcting, and training is to see transformed lives. We want to equip our people to be effective servants of the Lord Jesus Christ.

# Transformational Preaching

Not all preaching is transformational. Brian Mavis, a pastor and once the leader of SermonCentral.com, contends, "The overwhelming majority of sermons are informational instead of transformational. They hit the head but not the heart, soul, and strength."[3]

Let's look at the components of transformational preaching.

## Preaching Is Truth through Personality

The classic definition for preaching that Phillips Brooks uttered many years ago is *truth through personality*. Warren Wiersbe elaborates: "If your personality doesn't shine through your preaching, you're only a robot. You could be replaced by a cassette player and perhaps nobody would know the difference."[4]

Perhaps the most humbling aspect of preaching is that God wants to use me and you. He didn't place Billy Graham or Bill Hybels in your pulpit. He put you there because he wants to speak to your congregation through you.

## Preaching Is Proclamation of Good News

Transformational preaching is grounded in the gospel—the life, death, and resurrection of Jesus. Every aspect of a preacher's sermon should, in some way, relate to, proclaim, or apply Jesus' sacrifice to the life of the congregation. Otherwise, the preacher cannot claim to be preaching the gospel.

The way to test whether the Spirit has given you something to say is to examine how it relates to, proclaims, or applies the gospel. If it doesn't, you need to think twice about speaking it from the pulpit. The preacher's unique calling and platform is to proclaim the good news, the gospel.

## Preaching Is Bridge-Building

Transformational preaching builds a bridge from the time in which the biblical author lived to the time in which we live today. The first key to correctly applying Scripture today is to understand what the author intended to say and how those who first read the text would have understood it in their unique time and culture. Only then should we ask what it means for us today in our time and culture.

## Preaching Addresses Our Fallen Condition

People need to hear God's Word because we are fallen, broken individuals. If we had not sinned and were living in perfect harmony with Jesus, we wouldn't need to hear the message of God's grace. God's Word speaks to us in our fallen condition, offering forgiveness, healing, and hope. Transformational preaching identifies aspects of our lives where we need to experience God's mercy and healing. It also exposes our helplessness and offers God's grace. Many preachers feel the temptation to focus only on the positive and to avoid speaking about sin, brokenness, and helplessness. But when we have the courage to speak candidly about the need all people have for grace and healing, to address people's fallen condition, then we help God's Spirit pave the way for transformation to begin.[5]

## The Effect of Preaching is Cumulative

The effect of a pastor's preaching ministry cannot be judged by a single sermon. Transformational preaching has a cumulative effect.

A letter to the editor appeared in the *British Weekly*. The writer attended religious services regularly for the past thirty years and estimated he had listened to no less than three thousand sermons. Yet he could not remember a single sermon and wondered if a pastor might spend his time more profitably on something else.

That letter triggered an avalanche of angry responses that continued for weeks. Some letters criticized sermons and others defended them. Both clergy and laypersons took part in the exchange. Finally the following letter closed the debate:

My Dear Sir:

I have been married for thirty years. During that time I have eaten 32,850 meals—mostly of my wife's cooking. Suddenly I have discovered that I cannot remember the menu of a single meal. And yet, I received nourishment from every one of them. I have the distinct impression that without them, I would have starved to death long ago.

Sincerely . . .[6]

When a pastor with a shepherd's heart crafts and presents sermons, they have a cumulative, transformative effect. And God uses them to change lives.

## Exegetical Escorts

"Like Jesus on the road to Emmaus," says Robert Smith Jr., "preachers walk alongside their listeners, opening the Scriptures. Preachers are 'exegetical escorts' who usher people into the presence of God. It's not the preaching itself, but being in the presence of God that changes lives."[7]

If that is true, how can we be sure we escort people as effectively as possible? Here are some practical guidelines for preaching that transforms.

### Pray Sincerely

Your ministry cannot succeed—as God counts success—without prayer. Pray for enlightenment and for insight into the Word.

Pray for the congregation, that God will open their hearts and minds to the truth you proclaim. The Holy Spirit, who inspired the writers to record the Word, will help you proclaim it and your audience to grasp it.

### Plan Adequately

You would not hire a contractor to build a house if he showed up at the construction site saying, "I wonder what kind of house I should work on today." Neither should your sermon suffer from lack of planning.

Work toward planning for a series of sermons several months in advance. Then you can begin to jot down notes, form outlines, and collect illustrations well in advance of writing the sermons. By planning well ahead of time, you'll avoid the last-minute scramble of trying to throw together Sunday's sermon on Saturday morning. You'll enter the pulpit more confident, and your people will benefit greatly from the thoughtfulness of your planning.

## Prepare Thoroughly

If your preaching is to help transform people's lives, there is no substitute for thorough preparation. While every preacher develops a unique method for preparing a sermon, effective preparation always involves the following elements.

*Focus on the Text.* Rather than deciding what you want to say and finding a text that more or less supports your thinking, choose a text and ask what God might want to say to his church through this text. Remember that preaching is not about sharing your personal thoughts, but about presenting God's Word in a way that people can hear, understand, and apply. The easiest way to ensure you're preaching God's Word instead of your own opinions is to start by focusing on the text.

There are preachers looked upon by their people as divine oracles, who wag their tongues all day in light, frivolous conversation. Then before entering the pulpit . . . [they] seek a last-minute reprieve in a brief prayer. Thereby they hope to put themselves into the position where the spirit of the prophet will descend upon them. It may be that by working themselves up to an emotional heat they may get by, may even congratulate themselves that they had liberty in preaching the Word.

But they deceive themselves. What they have been all day and all week is what they are when they open up the book to expound it to the congregation.

—A. W. Tozer

In looking at the text, your primary responsibility is to determine, as best you can, its meaning. Use as many Bible commentaries and other reference tools as necessary to obtain a thorough understanding of the text.

*Connect with Your Congregation.* Pastors never preach in a vacuum. As you preach each Sunday, you are not preaching to all Christians everywhere, but to a specific group of people, with a unique history, culture, language, and perspective on life. Just as Paul's letters addressed the specific circumstances and situations of specific congregations, so your messages should be shaped by the common life and experience of the congregation under your care.

Let the knowledge you have about your congregation shape the way you develop each sermon. Choose your words, stories, examples, illustrations, and applications based on what will best communicate to, and connect with, your audience.

*Illustrate Appropriately.* Stories are the preacher's best friend. Not only do they hold people's interest, they can also communicate truth in a more powerful way than straight exposition or teaching can. However, it's important that the stories you tell be relevant to the text of your sermon. Each story should illustrate a particular point or the main message of your sermon; otherwise it's only filler material that is better left out. A great story in the wrong setting will only dilute the power of the sermon. Remember your goal as a preacher is to help people understand and apply the text you've chosen. If a story doesn't help you accomplish that purpose, leave it out.[8]

You can find material for illustrations just about anywhere. Your daily newspaper, magazines, television, and films will yield stories, quotes, and statistics that will help you illustrate your points. Be on the lookout for humor, drama, poetry, and anecdotes. Develop an alphabetical filing system in which you can drop clippings and ideas for illustrations.

*Answer the So-What? Question.* Application is, unfortunately, an aspect of preaching that few preachers give adequate attention to. My brother Terry, however, always includes a "So what?" section in every one of his sermons. Sermons only move from informational to transformational when you begin to answer the question: so what? What difference should this make in my life? Your sermon preparation is not complete until you know specifically what you want people to do differently as a result of hearing your message.

Application is hard work. If you as pastor don't take the time to think through how people's lives should be changed because of the message you're sharing from God's Word, most listeners won't go the extra mile to figure it out for themselves. And they shouldn't have to.

*Craft Your Sermon.* Some preachers prepare a carefully edited manuscript. Others find such a practice too constricting. But preachers who are consistently effective give attention to crafting their sermons. They pay attention to word choice, sentence structure, flow of thought, variety of communication and expression, pitch and tone of voice, dynamics, and on it goes. Achieving excellence in communication requires hard work, and typically it means reading through or even preaching the sermon several times in private before standing in the pulpit.

## Communicate Passionately

Your people will not hear what you have to say until they know that you believe it in your heart. In order to preach effectively, a pastor must communicate with authentic passion. As William Barclay said, "The listener will always know when a man believes intensely in what he says, and even if the listener does not agree, even if he thinks the speaker is misguided, he respects the accent of conviction."

There is not one correct way to communicate passion. Some preachers convey it through volume or animated gestures. Others demonstrate their passion with a quiet intensity. Again, the key is for your passion to be genuine. Your authentic passion will shine through in a way that is compatible with your personality.

Passion, however it is demonstrated, is essential for effective preaching. If you as the preacher are not deeply committed to the truth of what you're communicating, then those who listen will see no necessity or urgency to act on it.

## Conclude Proactively

Each sermon should conclude with a call to action. As I said before, every preacher must answer this question in advance: "What do I want the people to do as a result of this message?" As you come to the conclusion of your message, it is important to state or restate clearly what action you expect people to take, whether it be renewing their devotion, applying a particular principle, or finding an opportunity for ministry. Issue a clear call to action, so that people can have no doubt about the proper response.

A preacher with a passion to proclaim scriptural truth is one who is making a difference in the kingdom. People are drawn to fire. A pulpit ministry that is alive with truth, enthusiastically and carefully proclaimed, is one that will attract hungering hearts.

Gordon MacDonald confessed there was a time in his ministry when he paid less attention to the desired results of his preaching. Admitting this to his wife, he told her, "I'm not sure that anyone's going to change because of what I say. I need to remind myself to preach for change."

She paid attention to his confession. From that time on, when he arose from his seat next to her to go to the pulpit, she would grab his arm and say in a half-whisper, "Be a man sent from God; preach for change!"[9]

Salespeople use the word *close* to describe the moment when they ask a customer for a sale. Crass words for a preacher, but there does have to be a defined closure to a sermon, a clear description of the kind of response the preacher believes God expects. It has to be spelled out so that no one can escape the challenge.

—Gordon MacDonald

## The Fruits of Our Labors

Pastor Jim cringed as he saw Fred get in line to shake his hand following the service. He knew he would hear about the latest radio or television sermon Fred had heard. Sticking out his hand, Fred said, "Pastor, thank you for that message. I sensed it came from your heart. It really spoke to me and I do want to have a closer walk with the Lord. I'd like to buy you breakfast Tuesday morning and talk about it further, if that's okay."

Jim felt surprised and gratified to receive such a genuine compliment from Fred.

Even so, Pastor Jim has shifted his focus from competing with the superstars to being faithful to proclaim the gospel as God has uniquely prepared him to do in his own congregation.

## Action Steps for Preaching Effectively

1. Read or watch a few sermons from a well-known preacher whom you respect and appreciate. Study the preacher's method to determine what makes it effective.

2. Develop a filing system for illustrations, using alphabetized file folders into which you can drop clippings from newspapers, books, and magazines.

3. Listen to a recording or watch a video of one of your recent sermons. Without being too critical of yourself, note what you do well, and where you can improve.

4. Ask a trusted friend to provide feedback on a sermon you're preparing. Incorporate your friend's suggestions, where appropriate.

5. Form a discussion group with area pastors to share ways to effectively communicate in today's world.

# 5

# WORSHIP
## Modeling Passionate Devotion

*The pastor, more than any other person,
sets the tone for worship.*

P astor Mike rushed into the sanctuary with only two minutes
to spare. Lindsey had stopped him in the hallway to give him
updated information about the
women's meeting on Thursday
morning. Trying to refocus his
attention on the service, which
was to start in ninety seconds,

God calls us first to be a
worshiper, second to be a worker.
—A. W. Tozer

Pastor Mike opened his Bible to the Psalms. What was that verse
he had planned to use as a call to worship?

Finding it, he walked onto the platform and greeted the
congregation. After reading the verse and offering a short
invocation, he took a seat on the front pew and breathed a sigh
of relief. Just as he did, the worship leader called out the wrong
page number; his wife corrected him from the audience. Why
was he calling out the page number anyway? Normally, the

words are projected on the screen. As it turns out, the projector bulb had burned out just before the service began. Replacements are so expensive that a spare had never been ordered.

As the first song ended, the worship leader inserted a seven-minute commentary (with piano background) before starting the next song. Pastor Mike had been meaning to talk to him about keeping his comments brief, but hadn't yet figured out how to broach the subject without hurting his feelings. Chafing a bit over the song leader's feeble attempts at humor during one of his commentaries, Mike tried to rein in his thoughts and focus on the words of the song.

When it was time to pray, Mike fumbled in his worship folder for the notes he had made for the prayer. After pausing just a moment too long, he said, "Shall we pray?"

Finishing the prayer, Pastor Mike called for the ushers to receive the tithes and offerings, and returned to his seat. The offertory gave him an opportunity to glance once again at his notes for today's message. Meanwhile, he remembered the nursery director had requested additional help and he had forgotten to make an announcement. He would have to work it in right before the message.

Mike felt good about his sermon delivery, in spite of the teenage couple talking and flirting in the back row and poor Brother Jones, who always nods off in the second row from the front.

After the benediction, he greeted people in the foyer until the last parishioner had exited. He locked the door and walked to his car, thinking, *I led the worship service, but I don't feel like I worshiped today. I wonder if anyone could tell.*

Sound familiar? Most every pastor can relate to being so distracted by the details of leading worship that you wonder if you actually worshiped yourself. It is normal for pastors, especially solo pastors, to wrestle with this. All of us do from time to time. While we should always strive to be in the moment when it comes to worship, we should also not be too hard on ourselves when it just doesn't happen. God understands the unique challenges of leading worship while also trying to participate in worship. That being said, let's take a closer look at some of the potential distractions to worship and what might be done about them.

## Challenges to Worship

Halford Lucock tells about a doorman at a New York theater who guarded the stage door for seventeen years, but never once entered the theater to see a performance. Lucock asked, "Is it possible for a preacher and members of a congregation to become that sort of doorkeeper in the house of the Lord?"[1]

### Distracted by the Peripheral

I believe it is possible for us to become so distracted by peripherals, such as the mechanical aspects of worship, that we fail to focus on the central object of our worship—the living God.

How does this happen? How do we who are "professional worshipers," who are called to lead others in worship, fail to humble our own hearts during the worship service and set an example of true adoration and praise to God? One reason is that most pastors use the worship service as their primary method of disseminating information to the congregation as a whole. This includes making announcements about upcoming events, informing the church about ministry needs, sharing prayer requests, and other various types of communication. Many pastors underestimate the amount of time it takes to prepare to be the congregation's news anchor on Sunday morning. Then they are left hustling to gather and tie up loose bits of data to present in the moments before the service begins. Of course, that's also when they're most likely to receive word of breaking news. The stress created by the need to gather and disseminate all of this information can be a major distraction to worship.

Another peripheral that often distracts from worship is technology. Churches are incorporating unprecedented amounts of technology into their services, often greatly enhancing the worship experience for participants. But there is a dark side to the technology too. The more technology you use, the more preparation is required and the more that can go wrong during the service. How often do you find yourself anxious about the technical aspects of your service when you want to be preparing your mind and heart for worship? This is not to say that technology is bad or shouldn't be used in worship, but it does make worship more complicated and give pastors and worship leaders much more to think about during worship.

### Deprived of a Spirit of Reverence

Another challenge to worship is developing an appropriate spirit of reverence. The Bible often describes worship as being like the reverence offered to kings and other royalty. While no one can deny the many benefits and advantages to the spread of democracy around the world, it has had at least one disadvantage: fewer people today understand what reverence for royalty looks like.

Jack Hayford tells about touring England, Scotland, and Wales several years ago with his wife in a small rental car. Great Britain was celebrating the twenty-fifth anniversary of Queen Elizabeth's reign. They visited castles, admired the countryside, and soaked up the spirit of that ancient-modern country, which has so long been dominated by royalty. Hayford observed that, in England, the reverence and respect people have for the ruling monarch inspires people to have a sense of dignity about themselves. It was out of that experience Hayford wrote the song beloved by so many: "Majesty, Worship His Majesty."[2]

The one essential condition of human existence is that man should always be able to bow down before something infinitely great. If men are deprived of the infinitely great, they will not go on living and will die of despair. The Infinite and the Eternal are as essential for man as the little planet on which he dwells.

—Fyodor Dostoyevsky

Could it be that we have democratized Jesus, so that we are more comfortable calling him our friend than we are falling at his feet to worship?

## Rushing into the Presence of God

Madeleine L'Engle writes about a woman in Hawaii who described how her people used to sit outside their temples, meditating and preparing themselves for worship. When they finally entered, they would approach the altar respectfully to present their petitions. Afterward, they remained outside for a long time, "breathing life" into their prayers. When Christians came to Hawaii, they uttered a few brief words in prayer, said "amen," and were done. The natives called the newcomers *haoles*, which means "without breath." The Christians failed to "breathe life into their prayers."[3]

Too often we Christians hurry into worship without preparing ourselves beforehand, or taking time afterward to reflect properly. Add to this the fact that many solo pastors work in smaller churches where they do not have the resources for excellence in music, where change comes slowly, where congregants struggle over worship styles, where the atmosphere of the sanctuary resembles a family reunion more than a house of worship.

Add to this the fact that many people come to a worship service more concerned with what they will get out of it than what they will put into it. Many come completely distracted with the details of their lives—school assignments, work problems, home concerns, neighborhood issues, and relationship tensions. Others come out of a sense of duty or a sense of reluctant commitment to membership vows. Others come, mildly hopeful, but generally cynical about anything being different today than what it has always been.

It's no wonder that pastors often approach the worship service worried instead of worshipful, distracted instead of devotional, and focusing on the details instead of focusing on the divine. The good news is that it doesn't have to be that way! Before we look at some principles that will help the solo pastor lead effectively in this area, let's lay down a biblical foundation for worship.

## Biblical Worship

The psalmist exclaimed, "Let everything that has breath praise the LORD" (Ps. 150:6). In another place he declared, "Ascribe to the LORD the glory due his name; worship the LORD in the splendor of his holiness" (Ps. 29:2).

The Bible is clear. We are to worship the Lord and give Him adoration, for He alone is worthy of our praise.

## Old Testament Worship

Our Christian worship has been deeply influenced by ancient Israel's devotional practices. From the very beginning of time, one day a week, the seventh, was set aside for rest and worship, since God rested on the seventh day (Gen. 2:3). Keith Drury points out that early worship took place in individual or family settings.[4] No sanctuaries existed when Adam, Noah, Abraham, Isaac, Jacob, and Joseph worshiped. Adam and Eve experienced intimacy with God as they were "walking in the garden in the cool of the day" (Gen. 3:8). Both Enoch and Noah walked with God (Gen. 5:24; 6:9), which implies they worshiped him. All of the great patriarchs built altars, which served as focal points for their worship of God.

Later, when Israel became a nation, God provided specific instructions and patterns for national, corporate worship, first in the tabernacle, and then in the temple. It could be that the Hebrew people met for corporate worship while they were captives in Egypt. We don't know for sure. But we do know they worshiped God together at Sinai and then built a tabernacle—a portable worship facility—that could travel with them on the way to the Promised Land. Once Israel was settled in their new land and at peace, God permitted Solomon to build a permanent worship structure, the first of two Jewish temples, which became a national center for corporate worship. Animal sacrifice, full of rich symbolism, was an integral part of the tabernacle and temple worship.

In addition to offering sacrifices at the temple, the Jewish people also worshiped God through a regular cycle of national fasts and festivals, focusing at times on repentance, and at other times on celebrating the blessings of God and his mighty acts on their behalf.

Synagogue worship probably began during the Babylonian captivity and continued once the people of Israel were allowed to return to their homeland. In every village, synagogues sprang up and gave people the opportunity to worship together without traveling to Jerusalem. A typical service included readings from the Torah, the first five books of the Old Testament, as well as various prayers, praises, and an explanation of a passage of Scripture, roughly equivalent to a modern expositional sermon.

Besides all the great psalms that call us to worship God, the classic Old Testament passage on worship is Isaiah 6. The prophet tells us he "saw the Lord seated on a throne, high and exalted, and the train of his robe filled the temple." Around the throne were angels who called to each other, "Holy, holy, holy is the LORD Almighty; the whole earth is full of his glory." The scene produced a reaction in the prophet, who cried, "Woe to me! . . . I am ruined! For I am a man of unclean lips, and I live among a people of unclean lips, and my eyes have seen the King, the LORD Almighty" (Isa. 6:1, 3, 5).

William Temple said worship is to ". . . quicken the conscience by the holiness of God, . . . feed the mind by the truth of God, . . . purge the imagination by the beauty of God, . . . open the heart to the love of God, and . . . devote the will to the purpose of God."

## New Testament Worship

In the New Testament era, the worship of the early church shifted from the seventh day of the week to the first. After the resurrection and prior to the ascension, Jesus and his disciples were often together on the first day of the week (John 20:1, 19). After Pentecost, the newly formed community of believers regularly met on the first day of the week, presumably to commemorate the resurrection (Acts 20:7).

According to Gerrit Gustafson, biblical worship can be summarized in three statements:[5]

*1. True Worship Is Both Spiritual and Intellectual.* While we have houses of worship, we do not erect images of God to be worshiped. As Jesus told the woman at the well, "God is spirit, and his worshipers must worship in spirit and in truth" (John 4:24).

*2. Heavenly Worshipers Worship the God of the Past, Present, and Future.* The apostle John wrote that worshipers around the throne never stop day and night, saying, "Holy, holy, holy is the Lord God Almighty, who was, and is, and is to come" (Rev. 4:8).

*3. In the New Testament, God Endorses Three Primary Song Forms: Psalms, Hymns, and Spiritual Songs.* Paul wrote, "Let the word of Christ dwell in you richly as you teach and admonish one another with all wisdom, and as you sing psalms, hymns and spiritual songs with gratitude in your hearts to God" (Col. 3:16).

In a parallel passage, Paul wrote that we should "speak to one another with psalms, hymns and spiritual songs. Sing and make music in your heart to the Lord, always giving thanks to God the Father for everything, in the name of our Lord Jesus Christ" (Eph. 5:19–20).

These passages and others indicate that worship is not confined to a temple, synagogue, or church building. Worship is not restricted to a specific time or space, but can engage our hearts and minds any-

+>== ==<+

A silent love is acceptable only from the lower animals. God has given us speech that we should call upon his name. Worship is to religion what fragrance is to the flower.

—Henry Van Dyke

where and at any time. Worship involves praise, mutual encouragement, and the giving of thanks.

For a closer look at some of the key elements of true worship, we'll turn to Isaiah's vision of God in his temple.

## True Worship

Few would question that Isaiah's deep experience of God's presence or his humble submission was an act of worship. While our experience of God's presence may not be as dramatic as Isaiah's, it can be just as genuine and moving.

### Incorporate a Sense of Awe

When Isaiah saw the Lord, the Lord was "high and exalted, and the train of his robe filled the temple" (Isa. 6:1). Not only was God transcendent (high and exalted), but the expanse of his train speaks to us of his omnipresence. The entire picture evokes awe.

Unfortunately, we diminish the awesomeness of God in our minds when we talk about God, as so many now do, as our buddy. As Joseph Stowell writes,

If God were to show up visibly, many of us think we'd run up to Him and high-five Him for the good things He has done . . . or hug Him . . . or ask Him for an answer to that nagging theological question . . . or demand He tell us why that tragedy in our lives was permitted to rob us of our happiness and comfort. We would do none of these things. We would fall trembling at His feet as His awesome, mighty, and fearful glory filled the room.[6]

As you plan for worship in your congregation, make it a point to encourage a sense of awe among those who worship with you. Though we approach his throne boldly, we must never forget who it is that sits on the throne. True worship stimulates a sense of awe in the minds and hearts of worshipers.

## Recognize God's Rule over Us

Above the throne of God, Isaiah saw angels; seraphs to be exact. Each seraph had six wings and each set of wings had a different purpose. With two they covered their faces because they could not constantly behold the glorious face of God. With two they covered their feet, which were the only exposed parts of the angels. And with two they flew, or perhaps hovered, constantly available to carry out God's commands. Their presence in Isaiah's vision serves to underscore God's authority. The angels are his servants, and so are we.

Fred Smith says that one summer when it was 102 degrees in Dallas, he was asked why he went to church. He admitted that one August, during a very predictable sermon, he had written an outline for an essay on that very subject. The first reason, he said, is that Scripture commands it. The second is "that I needed it at least once a week to position myself under the lordship of Christ. He and I are not partners; we are not equals. I am subordinate. Sitting there in church each week, I recognize and renew the subordinate position."[7]

Your worship service should help participants understand their place in the universe. It is an honored place, only a little lower than the angels, but we are not the center. That spot is reserved for the Creator. True worship places God at the center and his people at his service.

## Offer Praise and Adoration

As the seraphs hovered above the throne, they called to one another, "Holy, holy, holy is the LORD Almighty; the whole earth is full of his glory" (Isa. 6:3). We can only give sincere praise and adoration to God when we see him as holy and ourselves as his servants.

In your weekly worship, give people every opportunity to express their praise and devotion to God.

## Confess Our Sin

When the seraphs sang, "Holy is the LORD Almighty," Isaiah saw that "the doorposts and thresholds shook and the temple was filled with smoke." This prompted the prophet to say, "Woe to me! I am ruined! For I am a man of unclean lips, and I live among a people of unclean lips, and my eyes have seen the King, the LORD Almighty" (Isa. 6:3–5).

A person who experiences God's holiness cannot help but recognize his or her own sinfulness. In contrast to the Holy One of Israel, we have to admit that we are far from holy. It's important for your congregation to have the opportunity incorporate worship to acknowledge and confess sins before God in heaven, and to hear assurance of God's offer of grace. Consider building into your service an opportunity for personal reflection and silent confession, followed by an affirmation of God's grace and mercy.

## Call to Service

After Isaiah confessed, an angel brought a live coal from the altar and touched his lips, assuring him of forgiveness. Then he heard the voice of the Lord asking, "Whom shall I send? And who will go for us?" Isaiah bravely answered, "Here am I. Send me!" (Isa. 6:8).

A firm conviction to serve God and accept whatever assignment he gives should mark every worshiper. As a part of every service, there should be some opportunity for the true child of God to say, "Here am I. Send me into the schools, homes, shops, factories, and offices of our community. Send me to those who need you. Send me to represent you in my world."

New Testament scholar Gordon D. Fee says, regarding worship, "You really should have this incredible sense of unworthiness—'I don't really belong here'—coupled with the opposing sense of total joy—'It is all of grace, so I *do* belong here.'" Fee adds that in too many mainstream evangelical churches, there is neither "reverence *nor* joy."

—Cited by Jim Cymbala in *Fresh Wind, Fresh Fire*

## Leading God-Honoring Worship

When people gather at your place, at your particular time, how can you be sure they have the best worship experience possible for that day?

## Drench the Service with Prayer

Many pastors spend multiple hours preparing their sermon for the weekend services, while spending only a few minutes thinking about the order of service. Spend time in prayer, not only about the message, but about the music, the prayers, the Scripture, the invitation, or closing. If others have responsibility for certain aspects of the worship service, pray for them and their preparation as well.

## Prepare for Worship

Few solo pastors have a worship leader who is responsible for planning worship. Thus, it probably falls to you to plan and think through every part of the service. Consider developing a checklist to go over as you prepare each service. Include items such as the following:

- Is the PowerPoint cued and ready?
- Are the bulletins printed and ready for distribution?
- Do the microphone units have fresh batteries?
- Has the sound technician done a sound check with participants?
- Is the accompaniment CD cued and ready?
- Are the Scripture readers prepared and have they rehearsed their passages?
- Has the worship team rehearsed?
- Have any special lighting effects been checked?

*Execute Well.* Talk with your worship team and remind them of the importance of their stage presence. Remember, a good voice alone does not qualify a person to serve on the worship team. Do they dress neatly and maintain good eye contact with the congregation? More importantly, do they demonstrate a genuine, humble approach to worship? Jeff Mansell says, "If you can't smile, if you can't look like you want to be there, if you can't inspire, you have no business being in a praise team."

> Prayer sensitizes us to the true meaning of worship. The person who spends time within the divine circle of companionship never enters the hour of worship without being sensitive to what can occur there.
>
> —John Killinger

*Eliminate Nonessentials.* Teach your musicians to make smooth transitions from one song to another, with minimal comment, to improve the flow of worship. Teach every participant to be ready to do his or her part at the appropriate time. They might move to the front row or just off stage so that the transition can occur quickly. Dead time—time when no one is leading worship—will not edify your congregation. Maintaining a good flow enhances the worship experience.

## Involve as Many People as is Practical

Leading worship does not have to be a one-person show. It is good to involve as many people as you can, providing they have the right attitude and perspective on participating in the service. Maybe you've noticed that your highest attendance usually comes on those days when several people are on the platform—when the children's choir sings, the drama team performs, awards and recognitions are presented. While you can't have a crowd on the platform every Sunday, you can intentionally involve more people in the worship service.

## Minimize Announcements

It's often necessary to make announcements during the worship service, but it's important not to allow them to disrupt the flow of the service. In most cases, it's best to briefly deliver any announcements at the beginning or end of the service. Look for ways to reduce the time spent in making announcements. If you have printed bulletins, you can make a brief reference to items that need to be highlighted and tell people they can learn much more in the bulletin. Many congregations now display announcements on their projector screens before the service begins. The key is to handle announcements in such a way that they don't distract from the purpose of the gathering.

## Lead Worship

By leading worship, I don't mean you have to be the worship leader. I hope you have someone else who does that well. But I do mean the following:

*Set an Example*. Be a worshiper yourself. Some pastors raise their hands during the congregational music. If this feels unnatural to you, don't feel obligated. But do sing. Even if you cannot carry a tune, you can mouth the words and set an example of involvement in the worship.

*Support the Worship Team's Ministry*. When you meet with your worship team or your worship leader, emphasize your belief in the value of their ministry. Also, help them understand your values for worship. Leaders are not there to entertain, to display talent, or to have a good time, although those things may happen during the course of the service. They are there to make it easy for others to worship.

*Be Clear About Your Agenda.* Be sure your worship leader knows the theme of your sermon. That way he or she can help the congregation focus on the theme through the music, Scripture readings, and any transitional comments that might be made.

*Affirm Your Team.* Many worship teams hear criticism more often than they hear praise. Take every opportunity to affirm your team. Let them know what a crucial part they play in leading the congregation in worship.

*Preach Like You Mean It.* A major portion of the worship service is given over to the sermon. Be sure your portion of the service is well planned and well delivered. Preach from your heart. Part of true worship is expounding the Word. Some people talk as if only the music is the praise and worship part of the service. In truth, all we do in the service should contribute to the worshipers' sense of God's presence, and their own response to Him.

> We should create the structure of our worship from the entire spectrum of songs—from ones written yesterday to those that are hundreds of years old—based on their godliness and ability to stir our spirits, rather than on chronology. I like the music of today when it meets this standard, and I don't when it doesn't.
>
> —Bill Gaither

## Standing Taller

A little girl sat with her father in a worship service. During the sermon she drew a picture of people coming to and going from church. The people coming in were short and stooped, while the people going out were tall and straight. When her father asked her to explain the picture, she replied, "When we go to church, God helps us to stand up straight and tall."

Pastor Mike did not feel very straight or tall when he left the worship service. The frustrating experience drove him to his knees. He asked God to help him as he analyzed the service and tried to determine how he could improve the worship experience.

Better planning helped him organize the announcements and prayer requests in advance. Putting everything together in one folder helped him feel more organized when he stepped to the platform. He began thinking of ways to share more of the worship responsibilities with others. He found the courage to meet with the worship leader and discuss ways they could improve the service. The worship leader took it surprisingly well and pledged to work toward a smoother flow. The next Sunday's worship experience was much better, and Mike continued to see marked improvement. It wasn't long before he too left the service standing a little straighter and feeling a little taller.

## Action Steps for Leading and Modeling Worship

1. Develop a checklist of things to consider before each worship service.
2. Plan a time to share your concept of worship with those who minister with you on the platform from week to week.
3. Consider elements of the worship service that are extraneous. Would eliminating them facilitate a better flow to the service? What can you eliminate next Sunday?
4. Evaluate how consistently each part of last Sunday's worship coordinated with the theme of the day. How could that be improved?

# 6

# TEAMWORK
## Transforming Committees
## into Ministry Action Teams

*A leader is a team builder.*

United Airlines Flight 232 was cruising at thirty-seven thousand feet when the number two engine, mounted on the vertical tail, failed. Its fan, six feet in diameter, sprayed pieces of fan blade through the right side of the engine housing. Shrapnel severed the hydraulic systems of the plane, making it almost impossible to control.

Miraculously, the crew maneuvered the plane for forty-five minutes after the hydraulic failure before it crash-landed just short of the runway at the municipal airport in Sioux City, Iowa. That date—July 19, 1989—will live in the memory of the survivors.

> No one can whistle a symphony. It takes an orchestra to play it.
> —H. E. Luccock

The crew that kept the plane aloft for so long, the rescue workers that saved so many lives, and the medical personnel that treated the survivors form a testimony to the value of teamwork. Without the teams that worked together—the crew, the disaster workers, and the medical personnel—the loss of life would have been far greater.

The mission of the church is no less crucial than the dramatic rescue performed by the various teams working the UA 232 disaster. The work you do as a solo pastor has eternal significance. The risks are high and the rewards so great that it is worth the investment required to develop ministry teams.

## Characteristics of a Team

Teams are different than committees. Committees are designed for discussion, debate, developing consensus, and making decisions. They're typically not expected to actually implement their decisions. When did you last see a committee hop up at the end of a meeting and begin working together to carry out their plan? That's just not the way committees function. Instead, they typically serve as legislative bodies and leave it to someone else to accomplish the real work.

Teams, on the other hand, are made up of people who not only debate, discuss, and decide, but also work together to implement their plan. Team members assume ownership of the mission and take responsibility for accomplishing the team's goals. While each team has a leader, leadership can also shift from one team member to another, as the situation requires. Teams also accomplish real work together, with each member contributing more or less equally.[1]

Unlike a standing committee, teams are created for a specific purpose. They dissolve or reorganize when that purpose is accomplished. People are not asked to commit to a team for a certain amount of time, but until a certain task or project is complete.

## The Rewards of Developing Teams

Imagine a disaster like the one at Sioux City and having no one, either on the plane or on the ground, trained to respond. In a sense, that's what churches face when they fail to organize effective ministry action teams. On the other hand, congregations that develop ministry action teams experience several benefits.

### You Share the Load

"Why do the same few people get stuck with all the work?" Ever heard that complaint? When congregations develop ministry teams, they tend to spread the work around much more. The reason is that teams are brought together around specific tasks that fit people's gifts and interests. More people can (and want to) be involved in ministry teams than committees.

Theodore Roosevelt wrote,

Like most young men in politics, I went through various oscillations of feeling before I "found myself." At one period I became so impressed with the virtue of complete independence that I proceeded to act on each case purely as I personally viewed it, without paying any heed to the principles and prejudices of others. The result was that I speedily and deservedly lost all power of accomplishing anything at all; and I learned the invaluable lesson that in the practical activities of life no man can render the highest service unless he can act in combination with his fellows, which means a certain amount of give-and-take between them.[2]

What Roosevelt described is teamwork. When we fail to work together, we wear out the faithful few. On the other hand, when we learn to work together and serve as teams, we share the burden.

### You Maximize Gifts

God gives every believer gifts for ministry and intends for us to use them. When we remain content for people to "sit and soak" instead of finding, developing, and using their gifts, we perpetuate spiritual lethargy. We allow God's good gifts to lie dormant in our parishioners.

Stephen Covey observed, "Dependent people need others to get what they want. Independent people can get what they want through their own efforts. Interdependent people combine their own efforts with the efforts of others to achieve their greatest success."[3]

When you involve people in ministry teams that fit with the gifts God has given them, you exercise good stewardship by maximizing the gifts of your congregation. In addition to helping your people grow and experience satisfaction in ministry, you'll also find that they energize others on their team.

### You Accomplish More

Teams accomplish more. It's that simple. Author and business consultant Patrick Lencioni says, "Most groups of executives fail to become cohesive teams because they drastically underestimate both the power teamwork ultimately unleashes and the painful steps required to make teamwork a reality."[4]

Forming teams does require an investment of time and energy, but so does trying to do the work all by yourself, or nudging the overworked into doing one more thing. The extra effort required to build and train ministry teams will pay huge dividends in the amount of work your congregation is able to accomplish.

Here lies a man who knew how to enlist the service of better men than himself.

—Andrew Carnegie's tombstone

## You Avoid Discouragement

Discouragement is the darkroom where fears and failures are developed. Some people are more prone to discouragement than others. However, even the sturdiest church member feels discouraged when only a handful of people are actively investing their time and energy in the congregation's activities. By putting together ministry action teams for various tasks, you help your most faithful and willing members avoid disappointment and discouragement.

## Biblical Teamwork

The Bible reports many examples of teamwork. David recruited his thirty chief men and his three mighty warriors (2 Sam. 23). Jesus chose his twelve apostles. Of the twelve, Peter, James, and John formed an inner circle. Gideon selected a team of three hundred soldiers, but only after God instructed him to reduce the ranks from the original twenty-two thousand (Judg. 7:2–8).

Solo pastors with limited resources may think they don't have the raw material to form great ministry teams. But remember the example of Gideon. Timid and fearful, Gideon was probably not the first person who would come to mind for an important assignment requiring bravery and courage. Yet, he turned out to be the perfect man for the job. Marauding bands of nomads from the desert areas of the Arabian peninsula—the Amalekites and the Midianites—had invaded Israel seven straight years. Riding on swift camels, they terrorized the land during harvest season. Remarkably, when God decided to appoint a leader to rescue Israel, he chose Gideon, who was hiding behind a winepress.

I'm just a plowhand from Arkansas, but I have learned how to hold a team together—how to lift some men up, how to calm others down, until finally they've got one heartbeat together as a team. There's always just three things I say: "If anything goes bad, I did it. If anything goes semi-good, then we did it. If anything goes real good, they did it." That's all it takes to get people to win.

—Paul W. "Bear" Bryant

Though secluded from the enemy, Gideon could not hide from God. Even Gideon recognized his lack of potential. When God called Gideon, he said, "But, Lord, . . . how can I save Israel? My clan is the weakest in Manasseh, and I am the least in my family" (Judg. 6:15).

## A Team May Have Hidden Potential

Gideon, who eventually became the leader, was like many potential team members—hiding in an out-of-the-way place, hoping not to be noticed, when he was capable of much more.

The angel of the Lord greeted him: "The LORD is with you, mighty warrior" (Judg. 6:12).

There's no evidence that Gideon had ever fought a battle, let alone distinguished himself as a great warrior. But God saw his potential.

## Teams Need God's Presence

God told Gideon, "I will be with you, and you will strike down all the Midianites together" (Judg. 6:16). Notice two crucial elements of that promise.

*We Need God's Presence.* Don't even think about forming a team without praying about it. God's presence makes all the difference in the world.

During World War II, Supreme Commander, General of the Army, Dwight D. Eisenhower, fell in step with the 30th Division Infantry. All seemed in high spirits as they approached their boats to cross the Rhine. Eisenhower noticed one young soldier who looked depressed and asked him how he was feeling.

"General, I'm awful nervous," said the young man. "I was wounded two months ago and just got back from the hospital yesterday. I don't feel so good."

When the general admitted he too was nervous, the soldier said, "Oh, I meant I *was* nervous. I'm not anymore. I guess it's not too bad around here."

Having the general with him made a significant difference. As leaders and teams, we too need the presence of our Commander-in-Chief.

> The important thing to recognize is that it takes a team, and the team ought to get credit for the wins and losses. Successes have many fathers, failures have none.
>
> —Philip Caldwell

*We Win as We Work Together*. God promised they would strike down the Midianites together. Even though he was the right man for the job, there's no way Gideon could have defeated the Midianites by himself. As President Lyndon Johnson said, "There are no problems we cannot solve together, and very few that we can solve by ourselves."

## Teams Need a Sense of Courage

Before tackling the Midianite army, Gideon was given a more easily managed task to accomplish. God instructed him to tear down the idols in the land.

Gideon and his small team of ten servants tore down the idols at night, "because he was afraid of his family and the men of the town" (Judg. 6:27). It was a first step that reminds us we don't have to conquer every fear perfectly in order to do something courageous. Sometimes we have to show courage in spite of our fear, as Gideon did.

## Teams Can Exert Positive Influence

Equipping his team of three hundred with pitchers, trumpets, and torches, Gideon instructed them, "Do exactly as I do" (Judg. 7:17). As a good team leader, Gideon coordinated their actions and set an example. The breaking pitchers, blazing lights, and blasting trumpets threw the enemy into confusion. They turned on each other and fled. Gideon led his men, and as a result, their victory provided an example for the nation, and the people turned back to God. Such is the power of a great team.

## Traits of a Team

Another biblical leader, Nehemiah, brought together a group of ordinary people and transformed them into an effective action team, rebuilding the wall of Jerusalem in a very short time. From Nehemiah's experience, we can learn a number of the traits of teamwork.

### A Team Works Toward a Common Goal

Teams are task centered. A well-defined goal unifies the team around a common purpose, guides the team's work together, and lets them know when their purpose has been accomplished. It is a common goal that brings a team together. When Nehemiah presented his vision and goal of rebuilding the wall to the residents of Jerusalem, they said, "Let us start rebuilding" (Neh. 2:18).

A poster caught my eye with its definition of teamwork: "Teamwork is the ability to work together toward a common vision. The ability to direct individual accomplishment toward organizational objectives. It is the fuel that allows common people to attain uncommon results."

### A Team Fosters Commitment

It was the day before the wedding. When the pastor approached the fellowship area of the church, he saw John spot-cleaning the carpet. No one had told John to do it. He was not especially skilled at carpet cleaning; he simply saw the need and worked on it. That's the kind of commitment that can be found in good teams. People jump in to help wherever they are needed because they care about achieving the team's goal.

Rarely do we have the luxury of focusing only on what we are skilled to do. A newspaper editor had just learned that a high-tension wire had fallen across a street in the middle of the business district. He assigned two reporters to the story, telling them, "No one knows whether the wire is live or not, so I want you to cooperate—one of you touch it and the other write the story." That will test your commitment!

Nehemiah assigned the priests to work on rebuilding the Sheep Gate (Neh. 3:1–3). I doubt they were particularly skilled at setting doors and putting bolts and bars in place. But they believed in their mission and were committed to accomplishing it, no matter what was required.

## A Team Uses Its Time and Talents

Nehemiah reported that while half the men did the work, the other half stood by with spears, shields, bows, and armor. Some "did their work with one hand and held a weapon in the other" (Neh. 4:17). Everyone contributed to the team's effort, though not everyone in the same way. Effective teams seek equal commitment, not equal contribution.

John Wooden, basketball coach at UCLA, led his teams to ten national basketball championships in twelve years. He said the key to success on the court was teamwork: "The guy who puts the ball through the hoop has ten hands."[5] Only one person at a time can score a basket, but everyone on the court plays a part.

Sometimes the solo pastor will be the one to put the ball through the hoop. Most often, though, he or she should be blocking or clearing the lane, or rebounding and giving others the opportunity to shoot. You win by developing and engaging the talents of all your team members. Buildings deteriorate, equipment wears out, and methods became outdated. The only asset in your church that appreciates is people. Given the right opportunities, your people will grow, develop, and add value to your ministry.

## A Team Accepts Praise and Criticism

One of Nehemiah's detractors smirked and said, "What are they building — if even a fox climbed up on it, he would break down their wall of stones!" (Neh. 4:3).

Criticism, ridicule, mockery — Nehemiah and his team faced it all, and they faced it down. It is much easier to maintain your confidence in the face of such opposition when you're working with your team as opposed to when you're working alone. As a team, you can encourage one another, remind one another why you're doing what you're doing, and believe together in the value and eventual success of your work.

Members of a team can also help one another deal in a healthy manner with any praise that comes their way. It's always good to have people who can help you avoid getting caught up in believing everything people say about you — whether bad or good. Teams

Pat Summit, basketball coach of the seven-time national champion Lady Volunteers of the University of Tennessee, said, "I have to focus not on myself or on what I'm feeling, but on what my team is feeling. So, as a coach, I try to empty myself of my own emotions, and I try to convey — through words, tone and body language — what my players need to hear." That's leadership — recognizing that the players are the ones who are getting the work done, that the coach's job is to affirm their innate talents and abilities that earned them a spot on the team in the first place.

can help us maintain a realistic and accurate view of ourselves amid both praise and criticism.

## A Team Cooperates Rather than Competes

Nehemiah reported that once the wall was done, his enemies "were afraid and lost their self-confidence, because they realized that this work had been done with the help of our God" (Neh. 6:16). Even his enemies had to acknowledge the spirit of cooperation Nehemiah had fostered in the people of Jerusalem.

Robert Boyd Munger tells about a young girl who ran in the Special Olympics. When the gun went off, she yelled, "I'm gone!" This was not an Olympic-form runner. She hit every lane. But she beat everybody by forty yards. Just before the finish line, she stopped and would not go across without her friends. When all six runners held hands and crossed the finish line together, she shouted, "We win!"[6]

For teams in the church, cooperation—not competition— wins the day.

## A Team Welcomes Challenges

Teams inspire confidence. People are much more likely to welcome (and overcome) a challenge when they're part of a team. Nehemiah's team knew the challenges they faced, and yet they "worked with all their heart" (Neh. 4:6). The King James Version says, "The people had a mind to work." Rather than feeling discouraged, they were excited by the challenge.

Edward Land, inventor of the Polaroid camera, said, "The only task worth doing is one that is well-nigh impossible." Impossible tasks, though, cry out for the assembly of a team. When you are faced with a challenge as a solo pastor, let one of your first thoughts (after seeking God's wisdom) be about how to assemble a team to meet the challenge.

## A Team Celebrates Success

The priestly tribe of Levi and the singers came into Jerusalem to celebrate with musical instruments and singing (Neh. 12:27–28).

Effective team leaders celebrate successes—large and small. Let your team members know you value their contribution, their cooperation, and their hard work by taking time to celebrate the team's success. When the task is a large one, be sure to celebrate milestones along the way. Celebration is key to encouraging your team and helping them remain focused on the job they've been called to do.

# How to Build a Winning Team

Since the best teams often initiate great friendships, let's put some practical guidance for building a winning team on the framework of this acrostic: FRIENDS.

## F—Focus on Relationships

A team is only as good as the relationships among team members. If team members are at each others' throats, or harbor bitterness or jealousy, you can forget about having an effective team. Focus on developing healthy relationships. Pay attention to how people treat one another and make it a part of your team's culture that every person is valued and respected for his or her contribution to the team.

## R—Renew our Commitment

Teams are made up of individuals who are committed to a common goal. Sometimes they are already committed before they join the team; other times they grow in commitment as a result of being a part of the team. Either way, effective teams require people who are dedicated to the task of accomplishing the team's mission.

## I—Invite to Participate

Someone asked John F. Kennedy, thirty-fifth president of the United States, if America's national sport was baseball or football. He answered, "The sad fact is that it looks more and more as if our national sport is not playing at all—but watching."

For too many people, church is a spectator sport. The committee structure of many churches places the focus on process. In other words, committees process information, hear reports, and generate reports with no expectation of any specific action.

Being invited to participate on a ministry action team gets spectators into the game. It moves them out of the bleachers and onto the field.

## E—Equip to Minister

Equipping the saints to do the work of ministry (Eph. 4:12) may involve some serious coaching. Authors Sue Mallory and Alan Nelson suggest these equipping strategies to transform a committee into a team:

*Be Sure Everyone Knows the Purpose.* Teams exist for the purpose of achieving a specific task. When they accomplish the task, the team disbands.

*Develop Responsibilities Based on Gifts.* Instead of putting square pegs into round holes or forcing people to work in ways for which they are not gifted, customize tasks based on abilities. This results in stronger motivation and greater effectiveness.

*Share Leadership and Responsibility.* A team does not consist of one leader and a bunch of followers, but a group of people who are each committed to the mission. Effective team leaders take the initiative to share leadership and responsibility with those they lead.

*Hold Each Other Accountable.* Establish benchmarks to chart your progress. Emphasize the timelines required for the team. Work together to accomplish the goals.

*Delegate.* A sports team with no coach may work in sandlot play. But in the work of the church, a coach is necessary. Oversee the work, delegate all you can, and chart the progress.

*Focus on the Biblical Importance of the Task.* Don't get bogged down with structure. Remember the team is working to accomplish something significant for God and the church.[7]

## N—Network the Body

The body of Christ has amazing resources to minister to one another. However, many do not know what the resources are. As we move among our people, we see how one person can help another. You may suggest a ministry to Mary because you know her giftedness would help Jane. Jane and her husband, Tom, may have the gift of hospitality that would be a blessing to a new couple. By connecting people to one another, you help them help each other.

## D—Demonstrate God's Love

Stuart Briscoe tells about visiting Chicago for the first time after coming to the United States from Great Britain.[8] Knowing he was low on gas but assuming he would find plenty of gas stations, he pressed on. Sitting with an empty tank on a freeway, with rain pouring down, he realized the fallacy of his assumptions.

> The freedom to do your own thing ends when you have obligations and responsibilities. If you want to fail yourself—you can—but you cannot do your own thing if you have responsibilities to team members.
>
> —Lou Holtz

An old, dilapidated car pulled alongside him. The driver said something in broken English and drove away. Fifteen minutes later, the man returned and filled Briscoe's tank from a borrowed gas can. Briscoe tried to thank him, but the stranger shrugged and said, "You look kinda new around here. Me, I just come from Puerto Rico on Friday. Ain't nobody do nothing for nobody in this city." Briscoe said it was "kindness in a rusty Chevy."

In a rusty Chevy or a new Buick, helping one another in the body of Christ fosters a spirit of teamwork.

## S—Serve with Gladness

Jesus said, "If anyone wants to be first, he must be the very last, and the servant of all" (Mark 9:35). Author Stephen Bly said, "Nobody wants to be servant of all. At our best moments, we'd like to be servants of some. As long as we can select the some."[9]

He's probably right. But when we decide to obey the Lord and serve with gladness, we discover great rewards. Such teams have unlimited potential for good and for God.

## Teams for Survival

The death toll from the crash of Flight 232 rose to 111 passengers and one flight attendant. Ten crew members and 174 passengers survived. Observers called the crew heroes because they were able to keep the plane aloft as long as they did and came so close to landing at an airport. With only fifteen minutes' notice, more than a hundred disaster workers had already gathered at the Sioux City airport at the time of the crash. Medical personnel streamed into area hospitals to assist the injured. The citizens of Sioux City gave blood at the local blood banks, while others opened their homes to accommodate survivors. People working together turned a tragedy into a tribute to teamwork.

Gordon MacDonald, writing about the crash, said,

The Sioux City model of competence, courage, and capacity for heroism was a glimpse, a microcosm, of what God originally made people to be all the time in personal sacrifice and teamwork. Not that every moment is a call to uncommon, life-risking action; rather, the call is to daily, routine nobility of spirit and servanthood. And that is not an environment for tame people.[10]

As a solo pastor, by sharing leadership and responsibility with ministry action teams, you can make a significant difference in the lives of your people, your congregation, and your community.

## Action Steps for Building Ministry Teams

1. Consider which committees in your church should be replaced by ministry action teams.
2. Make a list of needs that could be addressed by ministry action teams.
3. What are the obstacles to developing teams? How can you overcome them?
4. Consider which laypersons would function well as team leaders.
5. Spend time with lay leaders, talking about potential teams and the benefits they would bring.

# 7

# STEWARDSHIP
## Raising Funds for Ministry

*Stewardship is not about money. It's about managing
our resources to accomplish the mission.*

Pastor Dale's hands trembled as he approached the lectern
for the annual tithing message. Although he believed in
tithing with all his heart, he dreaded the responses if this year
was going to be like every other since he came to Ferndale
Community Church.

Hank would say, "Why do preachers always harp about
money?"

Sarah would complain, "With the
economy the way it is, you're lucky
we can give anything at all!"

Jared would say, "Tithing is an Old
Testament concept. It's legalistic to
stress that today."

It didn't seem to matter that
Pastor Dale's message was grounded in Scripture and reflected

Where your pleasure is,
there is your treasure.

Where your treasure is,
there is your heart.

Where your heart is,
there is your happiness.

—Augustine

the official position of the denomination. He never tried to lay a guilt trip on his parishioners, nor shame them into giving, nor lament the low offerings that left the church board constantly trying to scrape together enough dollars to make ends meet.

Yet he knew the complaints would come. His pulse quickened as he opened his Bible. Would he ever overcome the dread of this annual sermon?

## Why Stewardship Is a Problem in Many Churches

The U.S. Bureau of Labor Statistics for the year 2004 indicates the average income of American households, after taxes, was 52,287 dollars. Of this amount Americans gave away 92 billion dollars for charitable causes, including churches and other religious groups, other charities, educational institutions, and gifts of stocks and bonds. Giving away 92 billion dollars is impressive until you realize it represents an average of 794 dollars per household. That comes to about 1.5 percent of their income.[1]

The amount given to churches and other religious groups represented just over 1 percent of household income, far less than the Bible's teaching of a tithe.

Yet it is still the church that leads the way in giving to charitable causes. John and Sylvia Ronsvalle point out that "religion taught and promoted philanthropy in the U.S. and therefore is the foundation for the practice of philanthropy. These numbers add strength to that view."[2]

If the church, among all institutions, is the leader in giving, why do so many churches struggle with concepts of stewardship?

## Pastors Have Not Been Trained to Talk about Money

Some time ago, the *Planned Giving Today* newsletter published a survey showing that clergy lack skill in financial management. While they seemed to be satisfied with their roles as religious leaders, the vast majority felt their theological training did not prepare them to deal with stewardship: that is, the areas of administration, finances, and fund-raising.

## Pastors Are Stereotyped as Always Talking about Money

Perhaps, since ministers have not received adequate training in the area of stewardship, we have overcompensated by talking too much about it. Without question, it comes up every week when the pastor says, "Will the ushers please come forward to receive the tithes and offerings?"

And let's face it, congregations have not always been positive about this weekly ritual. Fred Smith tells the story of a pastor preaching about stewardship. "This church, like the crippled man, has got to get up and walk!"

And the people said, "That's right! Let it walk."

"This church," he continued, "like Elijah on Mount Carmel, has got to run!"

"Let it run, preacher!"

"This church has got to mount up on wings like eagles and fly!"

And they said, "Let it fly!"

But when the preacher said, "If it flies, it takes money!" the people shouted, "Let it walk."[3]

## People Have Not Been Trained to Be Generous

Paul Harvey tells about a woman who called the Butterball Turkey Company's consumer hotline and asked whether she could cook a turkey that had been in her freezer for twenty-three years. The customer service representative told her if the freezer had remained below zero the entire time, it might be safe but she would probably discover the flavor had deteriorated.

*Generosity is measured not by how much you give, but by how much you have left.*

The woman said, "That's what we thought. We'll just donate it to the church."[4]

That kind of "generosity" has long disguised itself as the real thing.

Contrast that with a young woman who sent her pastor a check for 435 dollars, along with a note of explanation. While she was in college she received a scholarship. She had never seen the money; it was applied directly to her education. After college, she earned the money to pay the tithe on that scholarship. She honored the Lord for what he supplied. Unfortunately, that kind of conscientious tithing is all too rare.

## Stewardship Requires Commitment

Pastors often have difficulty addressing stewardship because we know we are hitting people where they live—commitment. Some churches take great pride in not confronting attendees with issues of membership and stewardship. In other words, they never call the people to commitment. Yet both stewardship and commitment are a biblical expectation and requirement.

120

John Wesley became a wealthy man in eighteenth-century England. As his income increased, his spending habits remained approximately the same. In the first year, he earned thirty pounds, lived on twenty-eight, and gave two to the poor. In the second year, he earned sixty pounds, still lived on twenty-eight, and gave thirty-two to the poor. He continued living on twenty-eight pounds per year and giving an ever-increasing percentage to the poor. Later, when his income exceeded fourteen hundred pounds, he increased his living expenses to thirty pounds, and still gave away more than fourteen hundred to the poor.[5]

Anyone can look at Wesley's example with admiration. Most would say that his commitment to good stewardship was praiseworthy. Yet few in the church today (or throughout its history) can claim to live up to his standard. Most wouldn't even try.

How then can a solo pastor approach the issue of stewardship faithfully and realistically? Before we get to some practical principles, let's look more closely at what the Bible has to say about stewardship.

## Biblical Stewardship

While pastors may be reluctant to talk about money, the Bible never hesitates. By my count, Jesus talked about money in sixteen of his thirty-eight parables. One out of ten verses in the Gospels addresses money. The Bible devotes five hundred verses to prayer, less than a hundred verses to faith, but more than twelve hundred verses to money and possessions.

## Adam Was a Steward

Adam was a steward from the beginning: "The LORD God took the man and put him in the Garden of Eden to work it and take care of it" (Gen. 2:15). A steward is a person who manages something that does not belong to him.

## Abraham Tithed

Long before God gave Moses the Ten Commandments and established a written law, Abraham understood and practiced the concept of tithing. Four kings invaded the land of Sodom and Gomorrah, where Abraham's nephew Lot was living. The kings defeated the rulers of the area and carried away Lot and his family. When Abraham heard of this, he organized his servants and pursued the invaders. After routing them, he recovered the goods they had taken and brought back Lot, his family, and other people who had been captured. When Abraham returned, Melchizedek, king of Salem and priest of God Most High, met the patriarch and blessed him. "Then [Abraham] gave him a tenth of everything" (Gen. 14:20).

## Tithing Is Both Commanded and Commended

Malachi recorded God's command and promise:

"Bring the whole tithe into the storehouse, that there may be food in my house. Test me in this," says the LORD Almighty, "and see if I will not throw open the floodgates of heaven and pour out so much blessing that you will not have room enough for it. I will prevent pests from devouring your crops, and the vines in your fields will not cast their fruit," says the LORD Almighty. "Then all the nations will call you blessed, for yours will be a delightful land," says the LORD Almighty" (Mal. 3:10–12).

While tithing is commanded in the Old Testament, it is commended in the New Testament. Jesus said, "Woe to you, teachers of the law and Pharisees, you hypocrites! You give a tenth of your spices—mint, dill and cummin. But you have neglected the more important matters of the law—justice, mercy and faithfulness. You should have practiced the latter, without neglecting the former" (Matt. 23:23).

## Jesus Praised Sacrificial Giving

Jesus called his disciples' attention to a poor widow who put her money in the temple treasury. Others gave larger amounts, while the widow dropped only two copper coins in the offering. Jesus said, "I tell you the truth, this poor widow has put more into the treasury than all the others. They all gave out of their wealth; but she, out of her poverty, put in everything—all she had to live on" (Mark 12:43–44).

Medical missionary and Nobel laureate Albert Schweitzer said, "Whatever you have received more than others—in health, in talents, in ability, in success, in a pleasant childhood, in harmonious conditions of home life—all this you

John Wesley taught, "Make all you can. Save all you can. Give all you can." He went on to observe that all of his followers were excited about "making all you can." Most of his followers were enthusiastic about "saving all you can." But enthusiasm dropped off noticeably when it came to "giving all you can"! Frugality without generosity constitutes harmful hoarding.

—Wayne Schmidt

must not take to yourself as a matter of course. In gratitude for your good fortune, you must render some sacrifice of your own life for another life."[6]

## Jesus Made Giving a Heart Issue

Some sincere people think if we dedicate our hearts, the money will automatically follow. But Jesus saw it just the opposite. He said, "Where your treasure is, there your heart will be also" (Matt. 6:21). It's amazing, but true: the heart follows the treasure. Put your treasure on the altar of dedication and your hearts will follow.

John Wesley understood giving to be a heart issue. He said, "When I have any money, I get rid of it as quickly as possible, lest it find a way into my heart."

## Paul Commended Systematic Giving

Paul advised his disciples, "On the first day of every week, each one of you should set aside a sum of money in keeping with his income, saving it up, so that when I come no collections will have to be made" (1 Cor. 16:2).

Commenting on Deuteronomy 15:7–11, where Moses speaks three times of an open hand's being the result of an open heart, Matthew Henry said, "If the hand is shut it is a sign that the heart is hardened."

Whether people place a check in the offering plate once a week, every two weeks, or once a month, encourage them to give systematically. I have known farmers who would drop a large check in the offering once or twice a year, depending on when they sold their crops or cattle. But they did it regularly and faithfully every year.

## Paul Acclaimed Cheerful, Generous Giving

The Bible teaches us to give generously and cheerfully. "Remember this," Paul wrote, "Whoever sows sparingly will also reap sparingly, and whoever sows generously will also reap generously." Without addressing the issue of income, large or small, he added, "Each man should give what he has decided in his heart to give, not reluctantly or under compulsion, for God loves a cheerful giver" (2 Cor. 9:6–7).

God's blessings are not always monetary. I have known people who stepped out on faith to give extra, only to find their families were healthier during the next year, resulting in lower medical bills.

At the age of fifty-three, John D. Rockefeller was probably the wealthiest man on earth. Although he had an income of a million dollars a week, he was so obsessed with making money that he lost his hair and could only eat crackers and milk.

When he began to use his wealth to help others, his health improved. Dr. S. I. McMillen observed that "into the soul of John D. came refreshing streams of love and gratitude from those whom he was helping." Rockefeller lived until he was ninety-eight.

Robert G. LeTourneau, a Christian businessman and prolific inventor in the earthmoving industry, said, "I shovel out and God shovels in—but God's shovel is always bigger."

## Talking about Money

Talking about money in church is not just about dollars and cents. Giving should always be tied to the mission of the church. Nobody is motivated to give just for the sake of giving. A new building, a better children's ministry, a more dynamic youth program, a stronger outreach to the community—these are all worthy components of the church's mission. Here are some tips for talking about money that will leave people happy to give instead of harping about the pressure.

## Don't Be Intimidated

You don't need to feel sheepish when talking about money. You have the authority of the Bible behind you. If you ignore this topic, people will feel justified in using their money selfishly. You don't have to be a financial wizard. But you do need to teach tithing from a biblical and spiritual perspective.

## Tie It to the Big Picture

Don't be afraid to ask people to give to a great project. Robert Schuller said the roughest job he ever had was trying to raise eighteen hundred dollars for a dishwasher in the church kitchen. It was far easier to raise a million dollars for a building.

## Teach It as a Delight, Not a Duty

Be careful how you approach the offering time in your worship services. If you seem hesitant and lack confidence, you will communicate the wrong things. Nobody wants to invest in a shaky business. Avoid scolding, begging, and pleading.

Robert Schuller suggests, even when finances are tight, that a positive approach to the offering is always best. If his church was scraping to find the money to pay the bills, he said,

> Before the Sunday offering, instead of laying this weakness before the people and throwing *my problem* upon the tired shoulders of the persons who came to

church to *unload* their problems, I made a statement to this effect: "You people are wonderful. You come here week after week and give so generously, even though we never appeal and plead for your financial help. . . . There have been times when we were desperate for financial help. We prayed to God. We trusted Him and always He was able to meet our needs through wonderful people like you! I just felt this morning like I wanted to tell you how grateful I am, and how I love you for what you are doing! May God bless you! Thank you again. Now let us worship God with our tithes and offerings."[7]

## Use Testimonies of Others

People who have a positive testimony about giving will inspire others in your congregation to give. When you have them give their testimonies, you enlist other voices besides the pastor's in the important ministry of teaching stewardship.

## Set an Example

Be the first person to place a check in the offering plate. You are not doing this to be ostentatious, but to set an example. People need to know you practice what you preach.

Be faithful to lead your church in paying your denomination's assessments. This sends a clear message to your congregation

Without love, almsgiving is no more important an action than brushing your hair or washing your hands, and the Pharisees had just as elaborate a ritual for those things as they had for alms, too, because all these things were prescribed by law, and had to be done so. But love does not give money, it gives itself. If it gives itself first and a lot of money too, that is all the better. But first it must sacrifice itself.

—Thomas Merton

about the importance of being a team player. It also says, "We are not selfish; we do not spend all the money we collect on ourselves." Remember, it is God's money on loan to God's people to use for the work of the kingdom.

### Celebrate the Milestones

When you reach a financial goal, it's time to celebrate! Burn the mortgage after you make that last payment. Have a party when you reach your goal for missions giving or a capital stewardship campaign. Such festive occasions remind people that it pays to handle God's money in God's ways. God blesses an unselfish church that has a biblical strategy for raising and spending money.

### Connect Giving with Spiritual Vitality

Martin Luther observed, "There are three conversions necessary: the conversion of the heart, the mind, and the purse." Many discover the conversion of the purse is the most difficult and usually the last to be accomplished.

The way we use money is an indication of our spiritual vitality. When we hoard money, it indicates we do not trust God. When we waste money, it indicates we do not respect God. When people allow greed, miserliness, stinginess, covetousness, and materialism to consume them, these traits provide a window into the soul.

Don't be afraid to connect a person's attitude toward giving with the condition of their heart. It's exactly what Jesus did (Matt. 6:21).

# How to Fund Your Vision

Even though pastors may not have been adequately trained in dealing with stewardship issues, we have to do it anyway. Here are some practical ways to tackle the issue of stewardship.

## Connect Your Mission, Vision, and Values with Your Financial Needs

Giving is never just about the money. It's about the mission, vision, and values of the church.

Help your congregation understand that every appeal for funds is designed to advance the mission and vision of the church in a way that is consistent with its core values.

When people understand and agree with your mission, vision, and values, they are more likely to invest in your church.

## Build Your Church Budget Based on Ministry Priorities

Every church should develop an annual budget and base it on their ministry priorities. Here are my top ten tips for good budgeting:

1. Build your church budget with your vision plan in mind.
2. Structure your church budget to reflect ministry priorities.
3. Build a cash reserve equal to an average of one month's operations.
4. Build your church budget based on last year's useable income.
5. Monitor your annual budget performance monthly.
6. Provide monthly financial statements to your church board.

7. Seek church board approval for nonbudget expenditures.
8. Never spend more than one-twelfth of your given budget without special approval.
9. Give an annual written report to the congregation.
10. Celebrate by spending excess income on preapproved capital budget or projects.[8]

## Plan the Offering Time Each Week

The worship leader plans the music, the pastor prepares the sermon, but does anyone give extra thought to the offering time each week? If you approach it haphazardly, the results may be haphazard as well.

Why not use a brief drama or a video to highlight the importance of giving? A Scripture reading related to giving is appropriate. The witness of a layperson, reflecting God's faithfulness to the person who gave, inspires others. Positive stewardship quotes in the worship folder may encourage parishioners to give.

## Write a Brief Note to First-time Givers

If you tip a waitress 15 percent, why would you give God less?

—Jerry Brecheisen

A brief note to first-time givers, thanking them for getting involved in supporting the mission of the church, may reap dividends. Beyond any benefit we reap, however, it is simply polite to thank people who do the right thing. While they won't receive a note every week, a note after that first act of giving reinforces their decision to support the church.

## Open the Six Pockets of Giving through Systematic Offerings

Parishioners use at least six pockets of giving. It is wise to appeal to all these pockets regularly to give people a chance to respond to what touches them.

*Maintenance Pocket.* This is probably the hardest area for which to raise funds. There's nothing glamorous about maintaining the facilities. Yet it will appeal to some who know the importance of good upkeep.

> How can we expect our children to know and experience the joy of giving unless we teach them that the greater pleasure in life lies in the act of giving rather than receiving.
>
> —J. C. Penney

*Education Pocket.* Christian education strikes a chord with some individuals. They value the teaching of God's Word. They want to see programs that reach out to children, youth, and adults and encourage them to study the Bible systematically. Some will also want to support our church colleges and universities.

*Benevolence Pocket.* Feeding the hungry, clothing the poor, helping the homeless, visiting those in prison, and providing assistance to pay rent or utilities for the poor are all possible outreaches of the church for which people will give.

*Evangelism Pocket.* Others have a heart for the lost. They will give to see the church do more to reach those who do not know Christ.

*Building Pocket.* Many will be motivated to give toward a building project. A new addition, providing more educational or recreational space, a new sanctuary, fellowship center, or youth center—these are all projects that resonate with various people.

*Mission Pocket.* Others will want to expand the church's outreach to the unreached. Missions may include foreign or domestic ministries, through which we take the gospel to "Samaria, and to the ends of the earth" (Acts 1:8).

If you neglect an appeal to one of those pockets, there is no guarantee parishioners will give to causes represented by another pocket. Members who care deeply about missions may not be concerned at all about a new building. People interested in maintenance may not be interested in evangelism.

## Coach People on Money Management and Legacy Giving

The Duke of Wellington is best known for his victory over Napoleon at the battle of Waterloo in 1815. A recent biographer of the duke claims an advantage over other biographers because he found an old account ledger, showing how the duke spent his money. The biographer contends that is a far better clue to what the duke thought was important than all his letters or speeches.

What story would our checkbooks and bank accounts tell? Most people have never taken a course in money management. Perhaps this is why, all across the nation, families consistently spend more than they make. Many think and plan no further than the next paycheck.

Will Rogers used to say, "Too many people spend money they haven't earned to buy things they don't want, to impress people they don't like."

By offering a course in money management and legacy giving, you demonstrate that the church is not interested in simply taking people's money but is committed to helping them use their resources more wisely.

## Give an Annual Report to the Entire Congregation

An annual report spells integrity. It allows parishioners to see how the church has used the money they gave. It reminds them you have been responsible stewards. It also emphasizes your mission, vision, and core values because of the way you spent the money. It tells them the denomination is important to you because you paid your assessment in full.

## Spend One Month Each Year on the Subject of Biblical Stewardship

Four weeks is just the right amount of time to talk about the stewardship of time, talents, testimony, and treasure. It reminds your people that stewardship is about how we use all our resources for God and others.

You can assure them you will speak about money only in the final service of the series and you will not preach about money and tithing the rest of the year. Let them know you will present the church's budget for the coming year as well as a report of how the church used their money the previous year. At the end of the service, ask for a commitment. Provide a card that enables them to go on record as supporting the church with their tithes in the coming year.

## Freedom to Preach Stewardship

Fast-forward the calendar a year and it's time for the annual tithing message again. As Pastor Dale steps to the podium, his hands are calm and his pulse is normal. What makes the difference?

This year he put together a series of messages about stewardship. For the entire month he dealt with a holistic approach to stewardship. He spoke about the stewardship of time, the stewardship of talents, and the stewardship of testimony. The message on stewardship of treasure was a logical conclusion to the whole process. Although it was a stand-alone message, he placed it in the context of being stewards of all God has given us.

Each Sunday he had a layperson talk about how God had blessed in that particular area of stewardship.

Talking about money will always be fraught with some tension. There are always parishioners who don't get it. Yet Dale, like many pastors, has stepped up to the plate and is providing dynamic leadership for his church in this area. By being bold, yet compassionate, he will reap dividends for God and the church.

## Action Steps for Teaching and Modeling Stewardship

1. Compare your annual budget to your church's mission, vision, and core values. Does your spending reflect what you say is important?
2. Plan a series of messages on stewardship, using a holistic approach to the total stewardship of life, not just money.

3.  Who in your congregation would have a great stewardship testimony? With coaching, could they be persuaded to share it in a worship service?
4.  How long has it been since you celebrated some financial victory? What would it take to make that happen?
5.  Analyze your own giving. How well are you modeling your teaching about stewardship?

# 8

# OUTREACH
## Motivating Laypersons for Mission

*As the pastor's heart beats for lost souls,*
*so goes the heart of the church.*

Oskar Schindler, a member of the Nazi party in Krakow, Poland, watched as the Germans routinely rounded up Jews, murdered some, and sent others to concentration camps. A shrewd businessman, he amassed wealth producing enamel goods—pots and pans—and munitions for the German army.

He hired a Jewish accountant, Itzhak Stern, who encouraged him to employ Jews to work in his factory, since authorities shipped those whose labors were not considered essential to concentration camps. At first money motivated him. But at some point he became determined to help the Jewish people.

> The Great Commission is not an option to be considered; it is a command to be obeyed.
>
> —Hudson Taylor

By the end of World War II, he had spent his considerable wealth, buying and protecting the lives of more than eleven hundred Jews. At the end of *Schindler's List*, the motion picture about his life, he cried, "I could have done more."

Presumably, if he had sold his elegant jewelry, costly suits, and expensive car, he might have saved more from the gas chamber.

Many of us, looking at the lost condition of our world, may wonder, "Could I have done more?" Could we still do more?

This is the challenge of evangelism. By evangelism we mean what Jesus meant when he said, "The Son of Man came to seek and to save what was lost" (Luke 19:10). While some would rather not use the term "lost," preferring to call them "the people Jesus misses most,"[1] Jesus freely used the term to describe the people he wanted to reach.

## The Challenge of Evangelism

Perhaps no other word in the English language creates so much anxiety for Christians (and non-Christians!) as the word *evangelism*. You may become nervous yourself at the thought of sharing the gospel with someone one-to-one. You can be sure that the majority of the people in your congregation feel as much, and probably more, anxiety about talking to others about their faith. There are a number of reasons why evangelism presents a challenge, particularly for the solo pastor.

### "That's the Pastor's Job!"

Many people in the church, especially congregations with solo pastors, see the pastor as the professional Christian. They consider *ministry* to be the pastor's job, and evangelism most definitely falls in the category of ministry. They fail to recognize that God gave pastors to churches to equip laypeople to do the work of ministry. In order for your congregation to experience success in evangelism, that's exactly what needs to happen. But first, you'll need to overcome the mind-set that ministry is the exclusive bailiwick of the pastor.

## Finding a Method That Fits

The call of the church has never been to be political analysts. We're called to be cultural catalysts [who will act as] salt and light. But there are dangers. Salt, if you use too much, becomes embittering. If you sprinkle it, it flavors. Light is annoying if it glares in your face. . . .

I don't think Jesus called us to rub salt in the world's wounds, or to glare the light a foot from their eyes with a million-candlepower spotlight. He called us to be the warm glow of His love, and the flavoring quality of His nature.

—Jack Hayford

Perhaps you or others in your congregation have received training for evangelism in the past. In my era, we learned how to preach evangelistic sermons, give altar calls, and expect people to come forward to be saved. Then we entered a period where personal evangelism was strongly emphasized. Many of us learned to share the Four Spiritual Laws or some other personal plan of salvation to lead people to Christ one-to-one. More recently, friendship evangelism was the preferred way to reach people, by forming friendships, earning the right to be heard, and sharing one's faith in response to questions from the seeker. Today, incarnational evangelism is hot. Alan Nelson describes incarnational evangelism this way: "If your faith is worth having, I'll catch it by engaging in conversation and authentic community with you."[2]

The fact is that in order for any plan of evangelism to work it must fit the personality of the evangelist and the culture in which the evangelist ministers. It must be authentic and it must be relevant; otherwise it will repel rather than attract people to Christ.

## Biblical Evangelism

Mark Mittelberg says, "Each one of us has a biblical mandate to share the gospel, but that message should be filtered through the unique character-istics of the person delivering the message." In keeping with that idea, Mittelberg and coauthor Bill Hybels (*Becoming a Contagious Christian*) have identified six different biblical approaches to evangelism.[3]

Evangelism growth must be first. Transfer growth will happen. As our denomination continues to hold and declare tra-ditional biblical values, some people from more liberal settings will unite with us. . . . Biological growth should definitely lead to evangelism. Family evangelism should be the highest of priorities in our spiritual outreach. . . . Evangelism must be the driving motive behind all of our methods of outreach and Christian service to those needing the gospel. It can and will happen when we inten-tionally make it a part of all our church's ministry.

—Marlin Mull

### Peter's Confrontational Approach

Not everyone can use the con-frontational approach successfully. Not everyone has (or should have) Peter's personality. He was a straight shooter. Anyone who can try to correct the Son of God, as Peter did, has no problem speaking his mind. So it makes sense that God chose Peter to be his spokesman on the day of Pentecost. Boldly, Peter addressed the crowd and told them in no uncertain terms that they had cru-cified the Son of God.

This approach can work for people who are bold and who are addressing people who appreciate direct communication. A few people will accept an in-your-face presentation, but most will not. So be careful when you use this approach; be sure the Spirit of God is leading you.

## Paul's Intellectual Approach

Paul could be confrontational at times, but typically he gave a well-structured, rational presentation of the gospel. It's easy to see that Paul was an analytical thinker. His letters reveal a brilliant mind that could grapple with the great theological issues of sin, redemption, law, and grace. In Acts 17, Paul began by talking about the unknown god in Athens and then took his listeners passionately and rationally to the one true God, Jesus the Messiah.

Witnessing is that deep-seated conviction that the greatest favor I can do for others is to introduce them to Jesus Christ.

—Paul Little

Often a well-educated person needs a rational approach that might be too intellectual for others who prefer a presentation that is down-to-earth. Know your audience.

## The Blind Man's Testimonial Approach

In John chapter 9, we meet a blind man who is not identified by name. Jesus healed the man, but when the religious authorities accosted him, rather than being confrontational like Peter, or intellectual like Paul, he gave his testimony: "One thing I do know. I was blind but now I see!" (John 9:25). That was an effective approach because it was rooted in his life and experience.

A personal testimony is powerful because you and others know it happened to you and you can speak with passion and conviction. Such testimonies are often irrefutable. People can argue philosophy, creed, and opinions. But they cannot deny what you have experienced.

## Matthew's Interpersonal Approach

When we first read about Matthew, he is giving a party. "Then Levi held a great banquet for Jesus at his house, and a large crowd of tax collectors and others were eating with them" (Luke 5:29). Tax collectors like Matthew, though hated by many, developed significant relationships. Matthew's witness was powerful. This man who was probably known for his greed and stinginess was now displaying a warm generosity. He was sharing food and beverage as well as compassion and empathy.

The interpersonal approach is really friendship evangelism. Your friends trust you. You already have camaraderie with them. When you share the gospel, you are not starting from scratch. Instead, you are building on an established relationship.

## The Samaritan Woman's Invitational Approach

Jesus met a Samaritan woman at the well near Sychar. She had been married five times and was living with a man who was not her husband. Jesus introduced her to living water. Why would an immoral woman—and a Samaritan at that—have any credibility in that first-century culture? Perhaps her lifestyle made her testimony all the more convincing. People could see the change. Without being confrontational, she simply invited the townspeople: "Come and see." Many did so, and after two days of Jesus' ministry, they said, "Now we have heard for ourselves, and we know that this man really is the Savior of the world" (John 4:42).

As Elton Trueblood said, "Evangelism occurs when Christians are so ignited by their contact with Christ that they in turn set other fires." The Samaritan woman was so aflame for Christ that she did indeed set other fires in the community, resulting in many coming to faith in him.

### Dorcas's Service Approach

When we meet Dorcas, Luke has described her as a woman "who was always doing good and helping the poor" (Acts 9:36). Specifically, she made articles of clothing for needy people. She demonstrated love over time. As she served with compassion, she provided salt and light and made an impact for good.

She possessed a spirit similar to that of William Penn, who centuries later said, "If there is any kindness I can show, or any good thing I can do to any fellow being, let me do it now, and not deter or neglect it, as I shall not pass this way again."

To Rob Wilkins' list, let's add a couple more.

### Philip's Questioning Approach

Philip was proclaiming Christ in Samaria and experiencing great responsiveness when the angel of the Lord told him to go down the road from Jerusalem to Gaza. There he saw an official in the government of Candace, queen of the Ethiopians, riding in a chariot. When Philip came alongside, he heard the man reading aloud from Isaiah and asked, "Do you understand what you are reading?" (Acts 8:30). The man did not understand it, so Philip explained. He "began with that very passage of Scripture and told him the good news about Jesus" (Acts 8:35). What a delightful way to share Christ with another person.

As we walk the walk and talk the talk, our friends and neighbors may ask questions. When we take the time to listen and give them sincere answers, we too may see them come to Christ.

## Jesus' Personal Approach

Jesus, of course, was the master evangelist. We can learn much from his techniques. In addition to the methods mentioned above, Jesus excelled at dealing personally with individuals. He had the uncanny ability of meeting a person precisely where the person was. To the woman at the well he spoke of living water. To the fishermen he spoke of fishing for men. To the centurion he spoke as one with authority.

As we get to know people, we too will want to connect with them at the point of their needs. When we take an interest in what interests them, we create an open door for faith to flow from us to them.

## Principles for Evangelism

What principles should guide us in reaching others for Christ?

## It's About Lost People

Jesus had a heart for lost people. "When he saw the crowds, he had compassion on them, because they were harassed and helpless, like sheep without a shepherd" (Matt. 9:36).

Humanitarian Jo Anne Lyon tells about a sign hanging on the wall of a Lutheran guesthouse in Managua, Nicaragua. One of the first missionaries to visit there in the early 1900s placed it on the wall. It reads, "I came to Nicaragua to bring Jesus, and I found he was already here."[4] When we reach out to lost people, we are doing what Jesus came to do.

> Every Christian—as he explores the historical record of Scripture and tradition and comes to a deep, abiding faith—experiences that Christ is the risen one and that he is therefore the eternally living one. It is a deep, life-changing experience. No true Christian can keep it hidden as a personal matter. For such an encounter with the living God cries out to be shared—like the light that shines, like the yeast that leavens the whole mass of dough.
>
> —Pope John Paul II

## It's a Biblical Mandate

Jesus did not give the Great Suggestion or the Great Option. He gave what we know as the Great Commission: "Therefore go and make disciples of all nations, baptizing them in the name of the Father and of the Son and of the Holy Spirit, and teaching them to obey everything I have commanded you. And surely I am with you always, to the very end of the age" (Matt. 28:19–20).

Making disciples is broader than evangelism, but it begins with reaching people for Christ and then helping them become his fully devoted followers.

## It Can Be a Natural Extension of the Church's Webs of Influence

That's how Peter came to Jesus. "The first thing Andrew did was to find his brother Simon and tell him, 'We have found the Messiah' (that is, the Christ). And he brought him to Jesus" (John 1:41–42).

The question is, do we honestly believe that lost people are really lost?

On a Thursday in July, 1988, a three-year-old named Joseph Leffler was reported lost in the woods of northwest Oregon. Hundreds of rescue workers and volunteers combed through the forest while his parents waited anxiously for some word of their lost son.

On Sunday morning, Joseph walked out of the woods on his own and strode up to the coordinator of the search dogs. The headline in the newspaper read "Lost Boy Finds Searchers."[5]

For many years, that was the approach we used in evangelism. If lost people want to get saved, they must come to church. They must find us. Then we'll be only too happy to help them.

Webs of influence, on the other hand, emphasize our connection to people in natural ways. In a television interview, William F. Buckley said to Malcolm Muggeridge, "I would find it very difficult to talk to my compatriots about anything spiritual."

Muggeridge replied, "I find it difficult not to."[6]

Webs of influence take advantage of the opportunity to use natural contacts to touch people with the gospel.

> We are called to follow Christ onto our streets and into our neighborhoods. The outward journey, that journey which takes us beyond our own small world to the world in need, is the inevitable outworking of a genuine inward journey. The cross points in two directions—toward God and toward my neighbors.
>
> —Billy Graham

## It's a Way to Focus on Others Instead of Ourselves

In a parable Jesus taught, "The lord said unto the servant, Go out into the highways and hedges, and compel them to come in, that my house may be filled" (Luke 14:23 KJV).

Denominational leader Earle Wilson reminds us we must "go out after people." He says, "A church's good influence in a community may produce well-disposed outsiders who will remain outsiders until someone says to each individual, 'This is for you.'"

He tells about Oscar Wilde, who once wrote of his aunt Jane. It seems she "died of mortification because no one came to her grand ball. She died without knowing that she had failed to mail out the invitations." Wilson says, "This is the story of many churches that have wonderful worship services, splendid programs, and everything except a way of making some connection with those outside—those who always assume that the church is for someone else."[7]

## It Helps the Church Keep Its Focus

Jesus admonished, "As long as it is day, we must do the work of him who sent me. Night is coming, when no one can work" (John 9:4).

To keep our focus, we must avoid preoccupation with a specific method. As we observed before, Peter was confrontational, Paul was intellectual, the woman at the well was invitational, and so forth. As Mittelberg says, "Let's not lay guilt trips on people by acting as though if they really loved Jesus they would do it just like us."[8]

> Nothing is more important than reaching people for the Lord, yet it is easy to be distracted from our purpose. We need to stay focused on reaching one more for Jesus.
>
> —Rick Warren

Instead, let's find approaches that fit us personally and make sense in the light of the specific community in which we are located.

## How to Empower Laypeople for Evangelism

We have a duty and a privilege to tell people about Christ. As pastors, we have a responsibility to train our congregations in how to share their faith.

### Share the Responsibility

Professor of sociology Tony Campolo tells the story of Martin Niemoller, a German Lutheran bishop, who was called upon to negotiate with Hitler during World War II to see if he could convince the Nazi dictator not to close down the church of Germany. Niemoller told of a dream that recurred often toward the end of his life. In the dream, Hitler was standing before Jesus on Judgment Day. Jesus stood up from his throne, put his arm around Hitler, and asked, "Adolf, why did you do the ugly, evil things you did? Why were you so cruel?"

Hitler's head was bowed low. He answered, "Because nobody ever told me how much you loved me."

In telling that story, the bishop said he would always wake up in a cold sweat at that point in the dream. He remembered many meetings he had had with Hitler, but never once had he said, "By the way, Fuhrer, Jesus loves you! He loves you more than you'll ever know. He loved you so much that he died for you. Do you know that?"[9]

Sharing the gospel can seem like a huge weight of responsibility, as it did for Pastor Niemoller. But evangelism is not the responsibility of individuals alone; it is the responsibility of the church. Perhaps the greatest thing you can do to empower your church for evangelism is to share the responsibility. Focus on corporate evangelism. Ask, "How can we as a congregation best represent Christ in our community?" and "What role can you play in our efforts?"

> We are holding a light. We are to let it shine! Though it may seem but a twinkling candle in a world of blackness, it is our business to let it shine. Light dispels darkness, and it attracts people in darkness to it.
>
> —Billy Graham

Witnessing one-to-one is one method of evangelism, but a remarkably challenging one. Some of your people may have great success with it, others moderate, many little to none. We do our congregations a great disservice when we limit evangelism to one-to-one encounters, then make people feel guilty for not experiencing success with it. Instead, we need to tackle the responsibility of evangelism as a team.

## Find a Plan You Can Use with Confidence

When it comes to personal evangelism, each individual needs to find a plan that feels authentic and that can be used with confidence. Instead of choosing one plan and expecting everyone in your congregation to use it, teach your people a variety of ways to share the gospel when they have the opportunity. Then encourage them to select the one that seems like the best fit for them and personalize it.

The plan I have developed over the years is called "The ABCs of a Personal Relationship with Christ." My four-step plan is simple and mirrors the method Jesus used in bringing people to faith.

*Step One: Pray Beforehand that God Will Anoint You.* Prior to ascending back to heaven, Jesus told his followers, "Stay in the city [of Jerusalem] until you have been clothed with power from on high" (Luke 24:49). If they needed fresh power from God before undertaking the task he gave them, so do we.

*Step Two: Present the Plan of Salvation.* I patterned this plan after the way my Sunday school teacher led us to Christ when I was a preschooler. She said, "Boys and girls, receiving Jesus is as simple as ABC." Then she presented the following plan:

Admit that you have sinned. It says in Romans 3:23 that "all have sinned and fall short of the glory of God."

Believe that Jesus Christ died for you. It says in John 1:12 that "to all who received him, to those who believed in his name, he gave the right to become children and God."

Confess that Jesus Christ is Lord of your life. It says in Romans 10:9 that "if you confess with your mouth, 'Jesus is Lord,' and believe in your heart that God raised him from the dead, you will be saved."[10]

After I present this simple ABC plan of salvation, I like to use what I call the "how to get to heaven" pen. I always carry a pen that contains the ABC plan of salvation. Once I have explained that salvation is a gift, I like to ask the individual, "Would you believe me if I told you that I want to give you this pen?"

He or she almost always answers, "Yes, I would believe you."

Then I add, "But you don't have the pen right now, do you? What would it take for you to get the pen?"

"Well, I guess I would need to reach out and take it from your hand."

"That's right," I say, and hand the person the pen. "Now it's yours. Free of charge. No questions asked. It's the same with receiving Christ as your Savior. All you have to do is reach out and take him into your heart by faith."

*Step Three: Lead the Person in the "Sinner's Prayer."* I typically word the prayer like this: "Dear Lord Jesus, I know I'm a sinner. I believe you died for my sins and rose from the grave. I now turn from my sins and invite you to come into my heart and life. I receive you as my personal Savior and follow you as my Lord. Amen."

I am always moved when I see a newborn Christian look up from that prayer. The person is often radiant with newfound faith and filled with a sense of gratitude to God.

*Step Four: Give the New Believer Assurance that What Just Happened Is Real and True.* I like to use 1 John 5:11–12, which says, "And this is the testimony: God has given us eternal life, and this life is in his Son. He who has the Son has life; he who does not have the Son of God does not have life."

## Celebrate Encounters More than Success

Most pastors celebrate publicly each time a person makes the decision to follow Christ, and rightfully so. The redemption of a soul is a miraculous event and worthy of the celebration of angels. If you want to encourage your people to share their faith more, however, you need to celebrate the act of faith-sharing as much as, or even more than, a confession of faith.

The reason is simple: You and your people cannot control how many people receive the offer of salvation. You can control how often the gospel is presented. One thing is for sure: The more often you share the gospel, the more often people will receive it. Do you count baptisms in your church? Maybe you should count evangelistic conversations as well! By celebrating when people share their faith as much as when someone receives Christ, you demonstrate that your congregation truly values evangelism. When your people see how much the church values their participation in evangelism, they will be more likely to take the big step of sharing their faith. As you focus on encouraging the behaviors your people can control, the end result will be more lives redeemed.

## Saving a Soul from Death

Evangelist, educator, and pastor R. A. Torrey told about riding on a sailboat one day when the boom suddenly swung around and knocked a young man into the water. Torrey leaned over, caught him by the collar, and held him until others could help pull him into the boat. He had saved a fellow human being from possible death.

"But," said Torrey, "what is that to saving a *soul* from death. The life we save must be given up after all. One soul saved for eternity is worth a million lives saved for 10, 15, 20, or 50 years. . . . Natural death is in itself not such a dreadful thing, but the death of the soul is unspeakably awful."[11]

You can have great success in communicating to your people the tremendous urgency of our calling to share the gospel. As they see your passion and the value the church places on a single soul, they will respond to the challenge.

## Action Steps for Modeling and Teaching Evangelism

1. Prayerfully develop a personal plan of salvation you can use with confidence.
2. Consider who among your congregation are prime candidates to train for evangelism and outreach.
3. Analyze your worship services. Are people confronted with the claims of Christ? Are you giving them opportunities to respond?
4. Consider how you might train your children and youth workers to be appropriately evangelistic in their ministries.
5. Encourage your people to tell you when they have an opportunity to share the gospel, even if they didn't see immediate results. Praise their efforts from the pulpit.

# 9

# DISCIPLESHIP
## Producing True Followers of Jesus

*Teaching people to live like Jesus is an essential part
of the Great Commission.*

Judy Anderson grew up as the daughter of missionaries in Zaire,
known today as the Congo. As a little girl, she attended a rally
celebrating the one-hundredth anniversary of the coming of
Christian missionaries to that region. Of all the speeches, music,
and other celebrations, there's an event that she remembers most
vividly at the end of that day.

An old man came and insisted on
speaking to the crowd. He explained he
had information that would go with him
to his grave unless he shared it that day.

Leith Anderson, who related this
story, says the old man told how strange the missionaries seemed
when they first came to the area, then controlled by Belgium. His
people thought the missionaries' message was strange as well, and
they weren't sure they could trust the newcomers. So tribal leaders

> Disciples are not
> manufactured wholesale.
> They are produced
> one by one.
>
> —J. Oswald Sanders

decided to test the missionaries. Over time they slowly poisoned them. One by one the missionaries' children died. The old man said, "It was as we watched how they died that we decided we wanted to live as Christians."

That's a powerful story for a couple of reasons. First, nobody told it for a hundred years. Second, missionaries died strange, painful deaths, without knowing why they were dying. Neither did they know the impact of their lives and their deaths. What motivated them to stay under such circumstances? Why did they not go back home when the going got tough?

Obviously, they were committed to love and obey Jesus Christ and follow the call he had placed on their lives.

> The first and last word for a disciple of Jesus is "Obey!" I mean to say that the word *believe* is not as important as "You who believe, obey him whom you believe!" Of what use is believing if you cannot obey?
>
> —Johann Christoph Blumhardt

Is it too much to think we might, with the help of God, produce such disciples in this present age?

## The Challenge of Making Disciples

A small church in rural Kentucky took great pride in being a training ground for seminary students just beginning their first pastorate. While interviewing a young candidate for pastor, a member of the search committee described some of the former pastors who had gone on to serve in prominent capacities. One was the president of a seminary, another was pastor of a large city church, and a third had served as president of two denominational conventions and an international alliance.

The young candidate was impressed. He asked, "How in the world did you find that many potentially great men in this little church?"

"Find them?" the committee member said. "We didn't find them. We made them!"[1]

That's discipleship. When the church is at its best, it takes the raw material of broken human lives and, by the power of the Spirit, produces men and women fit for service in God's kingdom. The church that attempts to do so will experience a number of challenges, but with hard work and perseverance, you can overcome these challenges and become a disciple-making body.

## A Cultural Gap

Unfortunately, a significant gap exists between the culture of discipleship and the culture of our age. When looking for a church, few people today are looking for an opportunity to serve, to determine where they can have the greatest impact for Jesus. Now, many shop for churches as they might shop for a house or a car. Where can I find the best deal? What's in it for me? Trying to find the church with the best ministries for our children and young people is not necessarily wrong. But when people look for a church where they can remain anonymous and avoid serving in any way, it's hard to make a case that they're following Jesus. Yet that's what many are looking for in a church today.

> Christianity does not remove you from the world and its problems; it makes you fit to live in it triumphantly and usefully.
>
> —Charles Templeton

## Sunday School Struggles

In the early 1970s, more people attended Sunday school than worship services in some churches. Gradually Sunday school attendance has declined over the years. The problem is that, while Sunday school seems to be passing off the scene, it's not clear that there's another more effective tool waiting in the wings.

Author and professor Keith Drury cites several reasons why Sunday school has declined. His observations may apply to other forms of discipleship as well.

*Pastor Abandonment.* Although Sunday school used to be a port of entry to a church, the worship service has taken its place as the primary entry point. Many pastors do not even attend Sunday school unless they are teaching. What the pastor ignores often declines.

*The Trivializing of Sunday School.* Some churches have used campaigns, contests, and promotions to such an extent they seem to trivialize Sunday school. If it seems childish, adults may see it as second-rate and stay away.

*Small Church Crisis.* Many small churches, especially those with attendance of fifty or less, are struggling to survive, and that affects Sunday school. Some even drop Sunday school due to an inadequate supply of competent teachers, low attendance, and lack of interest.[2]

# Biblical Discipleship

The most effective disciple-maker of all time is, of course, Jesus Christ. The reason we even talk about making disciples is because he set the pattern for us and told us to "go and make disciples" (Matt. 28:19). Yet he did not invent discipleship. The Greeks were making disciples long before Jesus came into this world. Socrates, Plato, and Aristotle spent a great deal of time in public places, asking questions and engaging in dialogue with people sitting at their feet.

Jesus did these things as well, but, according to author and professor John Koessler, his methods of discipleship more closely resembled the Jewish model, which makes sense, of course, since that's the culture in which he was raised. Teachers of the Mosaic law, also known as scribes, gathered groups of learners who called their teachers *rabbi*. The learners often desired to become rabbis themselves. To this end, they studied Scripture and memorized the rabbi's teaching. They often walked a few feet behind the rabbi as a way of showing the teacher great respect.[3]

## Jesus' Method Resembled the Jewish Rabbis' Methods

Like the Jewish rabbi, Jesus asked questions as a teaching method. Although he taught the crowds, he often questioned the disciples in private (Matt. 16:13). He expected his followers to remember his teachings and assured them the Holy Spirit would help them recall what they learned (John 14:26).

He also expected his followers to obey his teachings. He told them obedience was a test of whether their love was genuine (John 14:23–24). Some of his followers ministered to Jesus, caring for his daily needs (Matt. 27:55). Like the rabbis who singled out one or two students to be their chief disciples, Jesus chose Peter, James, and John and allowed them to be with him when others were not (Matt. 17:1; 26:36–37; Mark 5:22–24, 37).

## Jesus' Method Differed from the Rabbis' Method

Although others referred to Jesus as "rabbi," he commanded his disciples not to use this title (Matt. 23:8–10). He cautioned his disciples not to think of themselves as great, but as servants (Matt. 23:11).

+⇒ ⇐+

I find that discipleship means, first, truly living. It does not mean a joy ride to heaven; it does not mean that there are no trials and no burdens. But it does mean peace in your soul and joy in your heart, and a sense, a supreme sense, of the smile of the Lord upon you. It is *living*. And discipleship means that you are using your time on earth to the best possible advantage. The Lord Jesus says so.

— William Culbertson

The rabbi's learners might serve as the teacher's personal attendants, but, in a complete role reversal, Jesus served the disciples: he washed their feet, a task usually done by a household slave (John 13:4–5), and he prepared breakfast for them on the shore of Galilee after his resurrection (John 21:9–13).

Jesus also differed from the rabbis by teaching with authority. The rabbis depended on the tradition of other rabbis who preceded them. But when Jesus taught, "the crowds were amazed at his teaching, because he taught as one who had authority, and not as their teachers of the law" (Matt. 7:28–29).

Jesus was willing to teach the multitudes, unlike the rabbis who usually taught a select few. Jesus viewed the crowds with compassion, while the religious leaders often looked at them with contempt (Matt. 9:36).

Jesus also accepted women as disciples. The rabbis typically regarded women as inferior to men. But Jesus pointed out Mary, who sat at his feet, as an example of one who "has chosen what is better" (Luke 10:42).

## The Apostles Made Disciples

We know very little about what most of the apostles did after Pentecost. But we know Paul made disciples. He told others, "Follow my example, as I follow the example of Christ" (1 Cor. 11:1). He became a mentor to Timothy and Titus (1 Cor. 4:16–17; 2 Cor. 8:17–18).

Like Jesus, Paul also experienced losses. Of the twelve who followed Jesus, Judas fell away (John 18:2). Of Paul's many disciples and partners in the gospel, Demas deserted him "because he loved this world" (2 Tim. 4:10). So we should not be surprised nor discouraged if we do not have a 100 percent success rate with our disciple-making efforts.

# The Making of Disciples

A disciple is a learner, one who is learning to live more and more like Jesus Christ. Let's look more closely at the essence of discipleship, and then how solo pastors, with limited resources, might help people learn to live Christlike lives.

## The Essence of Discipleship

Dennis Kinlaw identifies the essence of discipleship when he cites Jesus' statement to Peter: "Get behind me, Satan! . . . You do not have in mind the things of God, but the things of men" (Mark 8:33). In effect Jesus was telling Peter, "You need to learn to think the way God thinks."

If the essence of discipleship is to help people learn to think like God, the three laws of Christian discipleship, according to Kinlaw, are as follows:

1. Find out who Jesus is. Learn his adequacy for every human need.
2. Find out who you are. Realize your inadequacy for serving in God's kingdom, no matter how earnestly you try.
3. Find the Holy Spirit's power to displace your human weakness with the fullness of Christ.[4]

As we grow deeper in these areas—understanding Jesus, understanding ourselves, and replacing our weakness with Jesus' strength—our entire lives will change. We'll begin to think, talk, and behave differently.

## Developing Christlikeness

Paul's model of discipleship is found in 2 Timothy 2:2, where he wrote, "And the things you have heard me say in the presence of many witnesses entrust to reliable men who will also be qualified to teach others." In order to put Paul's model into practice, we need to determine what concepts, beliefs, and skills we want to pass on to those we disciple.

Author and pastor Steve DeNeff suggests five major categories to focus on in our efforts to develop Christlikeness in believers[5]:

1. Holiness—urging believers toward purity and integrity, especially in areas no one can see.
2. Discernment—helping people develop the ability to make wise decisions.
3. Perseverance—strengthening the resolve of believers to grow through adversity.

4. Compassion—encouraging believers to become sensitive to those outside the church.
5. Discipleship—working with others to pass these virtues along to them.

## Not a Technique, a Lifestyle

Disciple-making is not so much a technique as a lifestyle.

*Discipleship Works Best in Relationships.* Classroom instruction is important, but so is modeling and mentoring. Working through a set of discipleship lessons can be beneficial, but that in itself is not discipleship. Discipleship occurs in relationship, where we can discuss situations as they occur, share our own experiences, and pour our lives—not just information—into others.

*Discipleship Takes Time.* Jesus spent only three years in public ministry. The most effective thing he did in those three years, apart from dying on the cross and rising again, was pouring his life into twelve men. Without that experience with the Master and the subsequent infilling of the Holy Spirit, Peter, Andrew, James, John, and the others never would have taken the gospel beyond Judea, Samaria, and Galilee.

The apostle Paul's discipleship ministry with Timothy, Titus, Luke, and others continued for years. Initially, he discipled them in person, while they observed him teaching, preaching, and ministering. Later, he discipled them primarily through his letters. But all of it took time.

*Discipleship Involves Practical Work.* In addition to teaching his followers, Jesus also sent them out two by two and gave them practical experience. Simply loading down people with information, biblical or theological, is not enough. People need to have the opportunity to put it into practice in real life. Most often, this is where the real learning and growth occurs, as disciples learn to have faith in God in practical ministry situations.

*Laypersons Can Be Effective Disciple-Makers Too.* Laypeople can be highly effective at lifestyle discipleship. I remember godly laymen who set the example for me, took me under their wing, and mentored me. Pastors have trained me too, but I am a better person today because of the involvement of laypersons who loved me enough to spend time with me and be patient with me.

Author and professor Eugene Peterson tells about a businessman named Chet Ellingsworth, who functioned as his first spiritual mentor. Often this occurred, not in a restaurant or a living room, but in a duck blind, secluded in the marshes of the Flathead River.

"I can't remember him ever instructing me or giving me advice," says Peterson. "There was no hint of condescension or authority. The faith was simply there, spoken and acted out in the midst of whatever else we were doing—shooting, rowing, retrieving, or at other times, working or worshiping or meeting on the street and making small talk."[6]

## How to Build Disciples

Author and denominational leader Jerry Pence asks, "What is your church doing to lead believers to become 'fully devoted followers of Christ'?" To be more specific, he questions, "How are you turning spiritual babies into spiritual adults, spectators into worshipers, students into teachers, converts into evangelists, disciples into disciple-makers, church members into church planters?"[7]

## Three Kinds of Discipleship

Keith Drury cites three kinds of discipleship.[8]

*One-to-one Discipleship*. This is a relationship in which two people, one a more mature Christian, spend time together. It usually involves a Bible study or at least time with the Scriptures, sometimes using a formal lesson or book study. It may include thinking through and talking about spiritual concepts.

> Disciples are not manufactured wholesale. They are produced one by one, because someone has taken the pains to discipline, to instruct and enlighten, to nurture and train one that is younger.
>
> —J. Oswald Sanders

The key to the success of this kind of discipleship is the relationship between the two people. There needs to be a meaningful relationship in which one is helping the other grow to be more like Jesus. It may occur in a living room, over coffee in a restaurant, in a break room at work, or wherever the two people can arrange to meet. There is a high degree of accountability. It involves a great deal of time and energy to sustain this kind of relationship over time.

*Cell Group Discipleship*. This involves at least three, but seldom more than eight or ten believers, meeting together to help one another grow spiritually. As Drury says, "Christians purposefully meet in order to help each other become more like Christ." This type of discipleship also involves a great deal of accountability. People in a cell group often develop considerable intimacy and they have a strong commitment to get together and stay together to help one another grow.

*Group Discipleship*. Group discipleship involves a dozen or twenty, even thirty or more people—large enough to be a group but small enough to know each other. This may be a Sunday school class or a midweek group at church. It includes teaching, but also involves sharing and encouraging one another. There is intimacy, but it is not so intense that it frightens people away. This may be the most efficient form of discipleship because many people can be discipled in a relatively short amount of time.

## What's a Pastor to Do?

What should you do as a solo pastor? You should encourage all three forms. But don't try to do it all yourself. If you tackle one-to-one discipleship, I suggest you not meet with more than three people individually in a week. This is emotionally demanding as well as time-consuming. It is important work. But to be effective, you need help. You cannot disciple everyone alone.

> The nurturing and maturing of character, of putting off the old habits and putting on the new, takes a lifetime. And it takes place in the context of the community of saints, the church, through discipleship.
>
> —Charles Colson

Laypersons in your church can be effective disciple-makers. If you have a small church and you're not sure that anyone is truly qualified to build disciples, start with your most promising layperson. Begin with the individual you think has the greatest likelihood of continuing the discipleship process by eventually mentoring someone else. Remember that one-to-one discipleship relationships should never mix genders. Men should disciple men, and women should disciple women.

If you want to begin cell groups, you may need to form and lead the first group. Gather three or four laypersons and work with them yourself. By doing so, you will model this form of discipleship for the others in your group. Soon, some or all the persons in your group will be ready to lead their own cell groups.

Group discipleship may already be occurring in your church, especially if you have adult Sunday school classes. Be sure these classes include sharing and caring opportunities as well as time for a lesson. As people get to know one other, discover their joys and heartaches, and become involved in each other's lives, discipleship has a greater likelihood of occurring.

## The Basics of Discipleship

Jerry Jenkins, author of the Left Behind fictional series, tells about assisting Billy Graham in writing his memoirs for the book *Just As I Am*. Jenkins asked the evangelist about his devotional habits, specifically how he maintains his spiritual disciplines.

"There's no secret to that," said Graham. "God doesn't hide the key from us. The Bible says to pray without ceasing and to search the Scriptures. And I do that."

After probing for more details about his prayer life and his practice of searching the Scriptures, Jenkins said, "Say you miss a day or two. How do you get back to your routine?"

"Miss a day or two? I don't think I've ever done that."

"You never miss?"

Graham shook his head. "I told you. This is my spiritual food. I would no more miss this than a regular meal."

Jenkins went back to his hotel, thinking, "When people wonder why Billy Graham, among all those claiming the same passions, seems infinitely more blessed, more successful in his ministry efforts, they need to realize there is a difference between him and the others: We all know we're to pray and read our Bibles. The difference is, he does it."[9]

Most of us cannot say with Billy Graham, "I don't think I've ever missed a day." That's okay. Most of us can't hit a major league curveball or write a bestselling novel either. Even though Graham may be a spiritual superstar, we can still learn something from his passion for Scripture and prayer and his attitude that, if he can eat every day, he surely can pray and read his Bible every day.

Prayer and Bible-reading. Although it may seem basic, these are the very building blocks of discipleship. Sadly, they are also, apart from church attendance, the most neglected disciplines of the Christian life. But with patience and determination, you can make discipleship an effective part of your church's mission.

## Action Steps for Building Disciples

1. List the steps you must take to identify and enlist your most promising disciple-makers.
2. Do a study of the assimilation rate of visitors to your services, determining what percentage of first-timers, second-timers, and third-timers stay.
3. Evaluate the effectiveness of your adult Sunday school classes, midweek groups, and home Bible studies, measuring how well they incorporate new people.
4. Evaluate the measurable spiritual growth occurring in your small groups, with an eye toward improving real disciple-making.

# 10

# COUNSELING
## Helping Laypersons
## Find Wholeness

*Pastoral counseling and care make a difference for eternity.*

Swimming up from the depths of slumber, Pastor Steve gradually became aware that his telephone was ringing. He and his wife had an understanding. When the telephone rang in the middle of the night, she would answer and give him a chance to wake up, clear his throat, and get his bearings before taking the call.

When she handed him the phone, he glanced at the clock — 1:53 a.m. Theresa, one of his parishioners, said with a trembling voice, "Pastor, I'm sorry to bother you, but Tim just walked out. He's very angry and stopped just short of hitting me. I don't know if we can save our marriage and I don't know what to do."

> Pastoral counseling . . . is helping people resolve their problems, facilitating positive changes in their lives, and helping them grow toward greater wholeness.
>
> —Robert J. Morgan

Steve talked with her for a few minutes until she was calm. He prayed with her on the phone and made an appointment for her to come to his office that afternoon. He lay awake forty-five minutes, thinking and praying for Tim and Theresa, asking God to help them, and praying for wisdom for their appointment.

## The Challenge of Counseling

When the telephone rings at 2:00 a.m., it's never good news. Jarred awake by the jangling noise, a pastor immediately wonders who died, who's about to commit suicide, who's drunk and suddenly feels religious, or who is in jail and wants somebody to come with bail money. Having an unlisted home telephone number is usually not an option for solo pastors who must be available 24/7 to their parishioners.

### High Expectations

Crisis counseling is part of the solo pastor's job. So is marriage counseling, premarital counseling, grief counseling, occupational counseling, spiritual counseling, and general counseling. Pastors of large churches with multiple staff may have the luxury of referring people to a counselor whom the church retains. But solo pastors often feel they have to give parishioners an initial interview, at the very least. In reality, counseling is a part of every pastor's portfolio. Parishioners expect pastors to be compassionate, have a listening ear, and dispense wise counsel.

> Americans are desperate for a sense of community. Eventually many of these lonely people search for fellowship in a church setting.
>
> —James Dobson

Professor David Seamands says, "We live in a sick society that produces emotional cripples the way Detroit mass-produces automobiles. The Holy Spirit wants to work in people's lives; sometimes he needs a temporary assistant. That's the theological basis for counseling."[1]

## Prioritizing People

Many pastors, because they are computer-literate, fall into the trap of putting computers before the congregation, paperwork before people. This is not a viable option for anyone who wants to be an effective pastor.

Pastors are in the people business. In the business world, managers understand the priority of dealing with people and their problems. Authors Warren Bennis and Burt Nanus write, "What we have found is that the higher the rank, the more interpersonal and human the undertaking. Our top executives spend roughly 90 percent of their time concerned with the messiness of people problems."[2]

Hans Finzel, summing up the problem of putting paperwork before people, says, "When all is said and done, the crowns of my achievements will not be the systems I managed, the things I wrote, the structures I built, but the people I personally, permanently, influenced through direct contact."[3]

## Personality Disorders and Other Chronic Problems

Churches can sometimes be a haven for people with personality disorders and other chronic personality issues. Such people may never feel more welcome and loved than they do at your church. As it should be. Unfortunately, people with personality disorders and other issues can quickly become a major drain on the pastor's time and energy. Worse, unless you have a background in clinical psychology or a related field, there may not be a lot that you personally can do to help them work through their problems. Even competent clinicians experience limited success in treating some personality disorders. Unfortunately, it's often difficult for those of us who do not have a counseling background to recognize when a person should be referred to a professional counselor. We simply begin to wonder what's wrong with us that we can't seem to provide the help that's needed.

## The Problem of Transference

A major pitfall in pastoral counseling is transference—"the client projecting unmet feelings and desires into the counseling relationship, feelings and desires that belong somewhere else."[4]

Counselor Jim Newheiser observes, "Most people who seek pastoral counseling are women and most of them come because of problems in their marriages." When the pastor is a man, this creates complications for which the pastor must be prepared. Be sure you leave the door open or that the door to the room where you counsel has a window. Be sure your secretary or spouse is nearby, preferably in the next room.

Yet even these precautions do not provide total safety. A woman counselee may see in her male pastor all the good qualities she would love to see in her husband. The male pastor may enjoy the attention a woman gives him and the confidence she places in him. These are warning signs that spell danger if a pastor is not fully aware of what is happening.

Female pastors also face transference. They may be "the target of seductive ploys by certain types of males. These men are usually out to prove their masculinity; they see the 'pure' female pastor as a challenge to conquer, especially if she is attractive."[5]

## Potential Legal Issues

The area of pastoral counseling is one that is fraught with potential legal issues. Since many pastors are not trained or licensed counselors, it is easy for them to get in over their heads and to find themselves or their congregation in legal hot water.

Now that we've pointed out a number of the challenges related to counseling in the church, let's take a look at what the Bible has to say about counseling.

# Biblical Perspectives on Counseling

On the Bible's pages we read about great saints, great sinners, and a host of people between the best and the worst.

## Biblical Examples of Emotional Distress

I can't remember the professor's name, but I remember what he said: The four major emotions people deal with are anger, depression, joy, and fear. In other words, people can be mad, sad, glad, or scared.

*Anger.* Cain became angry when the "LORD looked with favor on Abel and his offering, but on Cain and his offering he did not look with favor" (Gen. 4:4–5). Had a counselor been available to Cain in those dawning days of history, might he or she have averted the first murder? In all fairness, God met with Cain and told him, "Sin is crouching at your door; it desires to have you, but you must master it" (Gen. 4:7).

Peter was impetuous. In the Garden of Gethsemane, he drew his sword and cut off the ear of Malchus, the high priest's servant (John 18:10). Paul, appearing before the Sanhedrin, lashed out in anger toward the high priest after the latter ordered that Paul be struck in the mouth. "God will strike you, you whitewashed wall!" Paul said. "You sit there to judge me according to the law, yet you yourself violate the law by commanding that I be struck!" (Acts 23:3). To Paul's credit, when he learned he was speaking to the high priest, he apologized.

*Depression*. King Saul was afflicted with depression and sent his servants to find someone who could entertain him with the harp and lift his mood. David came, "took an harp, and played with his hand: so Saul was refreshed, and was well" (1 Sam. 16:23 KJV). On other occasions, even David's skillful hand on the harp could not console the king. Although "David was playing the harp, as he usually did," Saul's anger and jealousy intensified. He "had a spear in his hand and he hurled it, saying to himself, 'I'll pin David to the wall.' But David eluded him twice" (1 Sam. 18:10–11).

*Joy*. On the other hand, David enjoyed a more cheerful disposition. Even though the people spoke of stoning him, "David encouraged himself in the LORD his God" (1 Sam. 30:6 KJV). He also wrote joyful psalms that exalt God and encourage us.

*Fear*. Fear is possibly the most common emotion we encounter in the Bible. The Scriptures refer to it more than two hundred fifty times. Many verses encourage us to put our trust in the Lord rather than giving in to fear. God spoke through

Isaiah, "So do not fear, for I am with you; do not be dismayed, for I am your God. I will strengthen you and help you; I will uphold you with my righteous right hand" (Isa. 41:10).

As pastor-counselors, we see in Scripture many examples of overcoming negative emotions and gaining mental and emotional health. No one is a better example of emotional health than Jesus.

## The Shepherd's Touch

The master counselor, Jesus knew how to deal with all kinds of people. Hans Finzel calls him the ultimate "people person." Finzel studied the Gospels, looking for leadership principles Jesus demonstrated. He discovered that "Jesus spent more time touching people and talking to them than in any other action." He called these actions of Jesus "The Shepherd's Touch."[6]

*He Knew Them.* "I am the good shepherd; I know my sheep and my sheep know me—just as the Father knows me and I know the Father—and I lay down my life for the sheep" (John 10:14–15).

*He Touched Them.* "When the sun was setting, the people brought to Jesus all who had various kinds of sickness, and laying his hands on each one, he healed them" (Luke 4:40).

> You can grow a dandelion in just a few hours, but it takes seven years to raise an orchid.
>
> —Richard Halverson

*He Healed Them.* "Great crowds came to him, bringing the lame, the blind, the crippled, the mute and many others, and laid them at his feet; and he healed them" (Matt. 15:30).

*He Affected Them.* "A student is not above his teacher, but everyone who is fully trained will be like his teacher" (Luke 6:40).

*He Mentored Them.* "I have set you an example that you should do as I have done for you. I tell you the truth, no servant is greater than his master, nor is a messenger greater than the one who sent him. Now that you know these things, you will be blessed if you do them" (John 13:15–17).

As shepherds, we want to imitate the example of Jesus.

## Principles for Counseling

Although most pastors are not professional therapists, they are expected to do some counseling. Here are a few principles to guide the solo pastor.

### Many People Already Know What They Should Do

Sometimes people need help in sorting out confusing issues and complex problems, but many of them know what they should do. They may be looking for an easier way. Or they may not see any hope in their situation. That's where we can help. We can offer hope, we can help them see options, and we can give them encouragement to do what they know they should do.

### You Cannot "Fix" Other People

A liberating idea for many pastors is that they cannot fix other people. It is not even our responsibility to fix them.

Our parishioners need to know we care. We must not fall into the trap of trying to fix everybody's spiritual and emotional problems. If we cannot fix them, what can we do?

## You Can Be a Facilitator

By getting people to talk about their problems, by getting them to think clearly rather than respond emotionally, you can facilitate solutions. You can help them begin moving in the right direction. Asking open-ended questions—which require more than a "yes" or "no" answer—is often helpful. You can discuss options with them. There are ways to facilitate finding a path to address their concerns.

## You Can Be a Good Listener

A newspaper advertisement in New York City invited readers to call a certain telephone number and, for a fee, someone would listen to what the caller had to say for a specific length of time. They would just listen, not tell the caller what to do. Before long, the number was deluged with calls. The lesson is simple: people seeking counseling don't need someone to tell them what to do as much as they need someone to listen to them without being judgmental. This is something the church can and should excel at!

## You Can Refer

Some problems are too deep for a person with limited counseling skills. You may find yourself in a situation where you feel you are in over your head. That's when it is helpful to know what resources are available in your community. Who has greater skills than you do? Referring early is helpful and may spare you the problem of getting in too deeply and finding it difficult to extricate yourself from a sticky situation that is beyond your skills. One caution: be sure you refer to a person who respects a Christian orientation; otherwise the counselor may make your parishioner's faith the scapegoat for all his or her problems. By the same token, a competent secular counselor is likely to be more effective than an incompetent Christian counselor. Don't assume you're making a good referral just because the counselor's ad in the phonebook contains a Christian symbol.

## You Can Use Counseling as an Opportunity to Share Christ

Carl Jung, the renowned Swiss psychiatrist, said, "Among all my patients in the second half of life (over thirty-six years of age) there has not been one whose problem in the last resort was not that of finding a religious outlook on life . . . and none of them has been really healed who did not regain this religious outlook."[7]

That comment comes from a secular perspective. But many pastoral counselors have found it to be true. A chaplain with many years of experience counseling alcoholics at a veterans hospital said he knew of no one who truly recovered from a life of alcoholism apart from a deep religious experience. Alcoholics Anonymous speaks of a "higher power." Why should we be surprised that people cannot cope apart from a relationship with Jesus Christ?

> If applied wisely and in partnership with Scripture, many psychological principles can lead people down discipleship's road.
>
> —Louis McBurney

Having said that, be aware that some people need more than spiritual counseling. Rusty Freeman said, "When people are having appendix pain, most of us pray for them *and* call an ambulance. So I wanted spiritual help *and* a mental professional."[8]

## Guidelines for Effective Counseling

God never intended for pastors to be Mr. (or Ms.) Fix-It for emotional disorders. Yet pastors can do a great deal of good by listening carefully and guiding people toward positive action.

### Develop Your Listening Skills

Listening well is important with the emphasis on listening *well*. Here are some tips on improving our listening skills.

*Look at the Speaker.* If you are doing other things—shuffling papers, catching up on other work—you will communicate that you're not really listening.

*Don't Interrupt.* Robert L. Montgomery says, "It's just as rude to step on people's ideas as it is to step on their toes."[9] Give people a chance to express themselves.

*Stifle Your Curiosity.* You may be dying to know more details, but if it's really important, eventually they'll tell you. Remember . . .

*The Presenting Problem May Not Be the Real Problem.* When counselees come to you, they may wonder, "Can I really trust my pastor?" They may be uncomfortable talking about the real problem, so they bring up a lesser concern to see how you respond before they trust you with the heavier issue.

*Focus on Understanding.* Studies have shown that most of us forget 50 percent of what we hear almost immediately. By the next day, we can recall only about 25 percent of what we heard. So it's important to be sure you understand what the person is saying.

*Determine the Need at the Moment.* Does the counselee want comfort? Understanding? Solution? Does he just need to vent? Is she relieving nervousness? Like the woman who just experienced World War III, counselees may simply want to know they've been heard.

*Check Your Emotions.* Look inside yourself from time to time to see if the person is triggering your own emotions. You need to remain as impartial as possible in order to understand and reflect accurately.

*Suspend Your Judgment.* Don't quit listening before the person quits talking or you may jump to the wrong conclusion. Responding before the counselee finishes telling the story almost always means you have made a premature judgment.

*Sum Up Occasionally.* If the person pauses, you can say, "So if I understand what you're saying, . . ." and then give a one- or two-sentence summary about what was just said. This ensures you are listening accurately.

What hurting patients need is someone who will honestly listen to them, understand their feelings, and not hasten to change the subject.

—Richard Exley

*Ask Questions for Clarity.* Earlier, I suggested you stifle your curiosity. There's a difference between asking to satisfy curiosity and asking to clarify something that is not clear.

*Make Listening a Priority.* Most of us preachers like to hear the sound of our own voice. It's an occupational hazard. But if we make listening a priority, we will be more effective as counselors. Roxane Lulofs says, "The feeling of being listened to is so close to the feeling of being loved that most people cannot tell the difference."

## Be Careful about Dispensing Advice

The problem with dispensing advice in your pastoral counseling is that people might actually follow it. If they do follow it and end up in worse trouble than before, they may be looking for someone to blame. Much better to listen, ask good questions, suggest additional options, and let people know that you want them to make up their own minds about what to do. In reality, that's the ultimate goal in counseling—not for you to dispense expert advice and solve all their problems, but for them to learn to think carefully and make good decisions about their lives.

## Maintain Confidentiality

Be careful in your preaching. Never use an illustration drawn from a counseling situation, unless you have specific permission from the counselee to do so. Even then, think long and hard about it. Nobody wants to become the illustration in the pastor's next sermon, and that might be what they think will happen if they go to you for counsel. Always get permission, and then be sure you tell your congregation that you asked for and received permission.

Jim Smith says, "As a pastor/counselor, I have essentially three things to offer the counselee: my unconditional acceptance, my trained insight, and an atmosphere of trust. If people can't trust me, I'm out of business. No one will confide in me any longer."[10]

## Counsel by Walking Around

You can save yourself hours of counseling appointments just by walking slowly through the crowd before and after worship services. In the hallways you can see people, shake their hands,

I don't respond to every squeaky hinge as if it requires a major repair job. One drop of oil can do wonders.

—Gary Gulbranson

look them in the eye, and be concerned about how they're doing. These simple contacts are all some people need.

If a person brings up an issue that requires counseling, you can offer to call him or her later. Sometimes a five-minute phone call will take care of a need without scheduling an hour-long appointment. By the way, if you promise to call, be sure you do!

## Set Boundaries

While pastoral counseling is a wonderful tool to help others, it can easily become the tail that wags the dog. The key is to set boundaries. Establish clear guidelines and limits so that your congregation knows what they can and cannot expect from you.

*Limit Your Counseling Load.* Counseling is not the only thing you have to do each week. But if you become proficient at it, it can soon overwhelm you. Professionals suggest we limit our counseling load to ten hours a week. This limitation contributes to your own mental health. If you exceed this limit, you will have trouble finding time to do sermon preparation, and you may not see your family as much as you should. If you find ten hours are too much, cut back.

*Set a Time Limit for Each Session.* If you let people talk until they can't talk any more, your sessions will be endless. Learn how to draw the session to a close after forty-five or fifty minutes. After an hour of talking, most counselees become repetitive. If they are not finished in an hour, set another appointment.

*Do Serious Counseling in Your Office.* All pastors encounter people outside the office. In a casual conversation in a restaurant or a place of business, people may begin to talk about their problems. If it's appropriate, you can offer a word of encouragement on the spot. But other situations may require more time. If you see the person is deeply troubled, encourage him or her to make an appointment and meet you at your office. This promotes confidentiality, the atmosphere is more formal and professional, and it is easier to keep time limits.

## You Are More Effective Than You Think

Sometimes ministers feel overwhelmed by the need and by what they perceive as their own inadequacy. Richard Hunt says, "Christian leader, be encouraged. You *are* doing a good job; the better you do it, the bigger it will become. Just remember *you* are finite; only *God* is infinite."[11]

## What It's All About

A new pastor was getting acquainted with the lay leaders of the church. One of them, a prominent businessman, said, "What this church needs is someone who will take care of the customers."

The pastor was not trained in business, but he quickly understood what the businessman meant. The goal of ministry is people. Over the next few months, as he began to call on people in the church, meet them in informal situations, and counsel with them in his office, he found them responsive to his pastoral care. Counseling those who struggled with various issues proved to be a valuable part of his ministry. As individuals became healthier, the church became stronger.

Andrew Carnegie said, "Take away my people but leave my factories and soon grass will grow on the factory floor. Take away my factories but leave my people and soon we will have a new and better factory."

It is not about our buildings and properties. It is not even about our programs, as beneficial as they may be. It's about people. Introducing them to Christ, helping them mature in faith, and facilitating their spiritual and emotional health strengthens the body of Christ.

## Action Steps for Counseling

1. Prayerfully examine your own emotions. How healthy are you in terms of managing anger, depression, joy, and fear?
2. Analyze how well your church is "taking care of its customers." If you are not doing this, who is?
3. Consider how many hours you have spent in the past month in counseling sessions. Too much? Not enough? If change is indicated, what will you do to address this?

# APPENDIX

## Additional Resources

**Chapter 3—Pastoral Care**
**Checklist for Selecting Lay Counselors**

For churches who want to train laypersons to be counselors, the question arises as to how to recruit them. Following is a checklist, which may initially seem rigorous and time-consuming. However, the experience of numerous pastors has demonstrated the value and importance of choosing counselors carefully.

_____ 1. A brief written statement acknowledging the applicant's adherence to the church's doctrinal positions.

_____ 2. A written testimony of personal Christian experience.

_____ 3. A written statement of the applicant's reasons for wanting to be in a lay counseling program.

_____ 4. A letter of recommendation from two or three people who know the applicant well.

_____ 5. An interview during which the class leader, other church leader, or pastor tries to assess the spiritual maturity, stability, and motivation of the applicant.

_____ 6. A psychological test or two, such as the Taylor/ Johnson Temperament Analysis (TJTA). Such tests have to be obtained and interpreted by a trained psychologist or other competent person.

Adapted from Gary R. Collins, "Lay Counseling within the Local Church," *Leadership*, Fall 1980.

**Chapter 4—Proclamation**
**Dynamic Analogy Grid for Sermon Application**

Whether the preacher's text is a verse, a paragraph, or a chapter, this tool helps the preacher move from the words and their meanings, to God's Word and his message for the people.

In the top row of boxes, decide what the passage says about humankind's need or problem, God's action or solution, and humankind's necessary response or obedience. In boxes four through six, put the text into a contemporary context. What are the needs today, what is God's solution, and what is humankind's response? In the last row, think of how the passage applies personally to your specific needs. This helps answer the question *Now what?*

|  | Humankind's Need or Problem | God's Action or Solution | Humankind's Response or Obedience |
|---|---|---|---|
| Then | 1 | 2 | 3 |
| Now | 4 | 5 | 6 |
| Me | 7 | 8 | 9 |

Adapted from David Veerman, "Sermons: Apply Within," *Leadership*, Spring 1990.

## Chapter 6—Teamwork
## Checklist for Finding Team Leaders

Use the quiz below to rate the potential of people you're considering for leadership roles. This is not a scientific quiz, but rather a tool to help you evaluate possible leaders in your church. Rank each person on a scale of one to ten in each area. The higher the score, the more likely the person is to be a quality leader.

| Characteristic | Score |
|---|---|
| 1. Trustworthy | _____ |
| 2. Humble | _____ |
| 3. Compassionate | _____ |
| 4. Patient | _____ |
| 5. Shows discernment | _____ |
| 6. Team player | _____ |
| 7. Ability to deal with conflict | _____ |
| 8. Ability to make beneficial decisions | _____ |
| 9. Desire to encourage development in others | _____ |
| 10. Understands and demonstrates priorities | _____ |
| 11. Attitude of openness | _____ |
| 12. Not afraid of change | _____ |
| 13. Demonstrates integrity | _____ |
| 14. Constant striving to improve skills | _____ |
| 15. Willingness to sacrifice | _____ |

Adapted from "Leading Minds" *REV!*, November/December 2001.

## Chapter 7—Stewardship
## Closing the Giving Gap

| Action | Technique | Advantage |
|---|---|---|
| Put an annual stewardship emphasis on the calendar. | Continually and consistently teach the benefits and blessings of giving. | Helps everyone have a handle on the importance of giving. Teaches it is more blessed to give than to receive. |
| Open the books. | Give regular reports on the church's giving. | Helps overcome fears due to recent scandals in the corporate world. Crucial to gaining and keeping faithful givers. |
| Develop the giving base. | Start stewardship training in the kindergarten class instead of the senior class. | Helps overcome the reduced giving base in smaller and mid-size churches. |
| Honor the committed. | Honor the stewardship commitments of your church members. Use sacrificial giving efforts as examples in sermon illustrations, while keeping giving amounts confidential. | Helps people understand that giving is its own reward. |
| Set the giving goals. | Set a goal that is challenging, yet attainable. | Helps a congregation focus on the future and avoid being stuck in the present. |
| Use giving models. | Use biblical models in your teaching and preaching. | Helps people understand that giving is biblical, not simply a man-generated method of financing the church. |

Adapted from Stan Toler, "Closing the Giving Gap," *REV!*, January/February 2006.

## Chapter 9—Discipleship

### Review Your Assimilation Strategy

Evaluate whether each statement is true or false for your church.

**T/F**  1. Our church has an effective way to welcome people that does not embarrass them.

**T/F**  2. Our church has entry level positions of service available to new people.

**T/F**  4. Our church has a purpose statement of twenty-five words or less that people have memorized.

**T/F**  5. Our church has a Christian education curriculum that meets the felt needs of the congregation.

**T/F**  6. Our church has regular socials especially to help new members make friends.

**T/F**  7. Our church has a way to help new people discover and use their gifts.

**T/F**  8. Our church has started at least two new small groups in the last year.

**T/F**  9. Our church has a vision for the future that people understand and by which they are challenged.

**T/F** 11. Our church people can identify a minimum of seven friends in our church.

**T/F** 12. Our church has an involvement level of at least 60 percent.

**T/F** 13. Our church has a variety of small groups available.

**T/F** 15. Our people sense they are growing spiritually.

1–4 T's = Poor; overall unbalanced strategy
5–8 T's = Good; strong in some areas, weak in others
9–12 T's = Excellent; overall balanced strategy

Adapted from Gary McIntosh and Glen Martin, *Finding Them, Keeping Them* (Nashville: Broadman Press, 1992).

# NOTES

**Chapter One**

1. Matthew Schofield, *The Kansas City Star*, April 2, 1997, A-1.
2. Cited by J. Oswald Sanders, *Spiritual Leadership* (Chicago: Moody Press, 1967), 94.
3. Billy Graham and Joan Winmill Brown, "January 2" in *Day by Day with Billy Graham* (Charlotte, N.C.: BGEA, 1976).
4. Jim Collins, "Best New Year's Resolution? A 'Stop Doing' List," http://www.jimcollins.com/lib/articles/12_03.html (accessed June 12, 2008).
5. Chuck Swindoll, "Model the Master," *Stimulus*, Spring 1996, 1–2.
6. Alan Nelson, "How to Get it All Done," *REV!*, May/June 2006, 60.
7. Sue Mallory, "The Art of Equipping," *REV!*, January/February 2006, 90.
8. Nelson, 56–57.

**Chapter Two**

1. Craig Brian Larson, "Brown-Out," http://www.ctlibrary.com/6117, accessed January 16, 2008.
2. Christianity Today International, "The Work Week of a Pastor," http://www.buildingchurchleaders.com/downloads/churchresearc/ cr05.html, accessed January 18, 2008.
3. "Servant Leaders," *REV!*, January/February 2006, 30.
4. Cited by Fred Smith, *Learning to Lead* (Dallas: Word, 1986), 41–42.
5. Jack Welch, *Winning* (New York: HarperCollins, 2005), 61.
6. Robert Black and Ronald McClung, *1 & 2 Timothy, Titus, Philemon* (Indianapolis, Ind.: Wesleyan, 2004), 36.
7. Waylon Moore, "Mentoring: Accelerating Leadership Growth," http://www.mentoring-disciples.org/growth.html, accessed January 18, 2008.

8. Cited by J. Oswald Sanders, *Spiritual Leadership* (Chicago: Moody Press, 1967), 179.

9. Bobb Biehl, *Dream Energy* (Mt. Dora, Fla.: Quick Wisdom Publishing, 2001), 261.

**Chapter Three**

1. Cited by Doug Self, *Mastering Pastoral Care* (Portland, Ore.: Multnomah, 1990), 20.

2. Stan Toler, *Stan Toler's Practical Guide for Pastoral Ministry* (Indianapolis, Ind.: Wesleyan, 2006), 103.

3. Roger L. Hahn, *Matthew: A Commentary for Bible Students* (Indianapolis, Ind.: Wesleyan, 2007), 131.

4. D. Michael Lindsay, "Creating a Culture of Connectivity," *REV!*, March/April 2005, 55.

5. Cited by Lee Strobel, *God's Outrageous Claims* (Grand Rapids, Mich.: Zondervan, 1997), 121.

6. Robert J. Morgan, "Why Pastors Make Great Counselors," *Building Your Church Through Counsel and Care* (Minneapolis, Minn.: Bethany, 1997), 67ff.

7. Tony Morgan and Tim Stevens, "Need Volunteers—Don't Ask!" *REV!*, March/April 2005, 70.

**Chapter Four**

1. Cited in James D. Berkley, ed., *Preaching to Convince* (Waco, Tex.: Word, 1986), 45.

2. Cited by Bill Bennett, *Thirty Minutes to Raise the Dead* (Nashville: Nelson, 1991), 162.

3. Brian Mavis, "30,000 Sermons Don't Lie," *REV!*, September/October 2006, 88.

4. Warren Wiersbe, "Your Preaching is Unique," *Leadership*, Summer 1981, 32–34.

5. See Bryan Chapell, *Christ-Centered Preaching: Redeeming the Expository Sermon* (Grand Rapids, Mich.: Baker, 1994).

6. Berkley, 11.

7. "What Gives Preaching Its Power?" *Leadership*, Spring 2004, 30.

8. For more on effective use of illustrations, see Bryan Chapell, *Using Illustrations to Preach with Power* (Wheaton, Ill.: Crossway, 2001).

9. Gordon MacDonald, "Soul Deep," *Leadership*, Spring 2004, 52.

**Chapter Five**

1. Cited by Gordon MacDonald, *Forging a Real World Faith* (Nashville: Nelson, 1989), 113.

2. Jack Hayford, *Worship His Majesty* (Waco, Tex.: Word, 1987), 9–14.

3. Cited by MacDonald, 60.

4. Keith Drury, *The Wonder of Worship* (Indianapolis, Ind.: Wesleyan, 2002), 211–214.

5. Gerrit Gustafson, "Psalms, Hymns, and Spiritual Songs," *Worship Leader*, May/June 1996, 35.

6. Joseph M. Stowell, "Is God Cute, or What?" *Moody*, November/December 1997, 6.

7. Fred Smith, *Learning to Lead* (Dallas: Word, 1986), 157.

**Chapter Six**

1. John R. Katzenbach, *Teams at the Top* (Boston: HBS, 1998), 15.

2. Roosevelt, Theodore, *An Autobiography* (New York: Da Capo, 1985), 86.

3. Stephen R. Covey, *The 7 Habits of Highly Effective People* (New York: Simon & Schuster, 1990), 49.

4. Patrick Lenioni, "The Trouble with Teamwork," http://www.tablegroup.com/pat/articles/article/?id=5, accessed August 19, 2008.

5. Cited by John Maxwell, "Why Leaders Need to Reproduce Leaders," *Equipping the Saints*, 1st Quarter 1995, 14–16.

6. Robert Boyd Munger, *Leading From the Heart* (Downers Grove, Ill.: InterVarsity, 1995), 67.

7. Sue Mallory and Alan Nelson, "The Equipping Church: Pastors and Parishioners Side by Side," *REV!*, September/October 2001, 50.

8. Stuart Briscoe, "Nobody Helps Nobody," http://www.christianitytoday.com/moi/2001/003/jun/11.11.html, accessed August 19, 2008.

9. Stephen Bly, "Leading from the Back of the Line," *Moody*, Nov–Dec 2001, 24.

10. Gordon MacDonald, *Forging a Real World Faith* (Nashville: Nelson, 1989), 168.

**Chapter Seven**

1. Cited by Joel Belz, "Stingy Givers," *World*, June 24, 2006, 4.

2. Ibid.

3. Fred Smith, *Learning to Lead* (Dallas: Word, 1986), 21–22.

4. Cited in *Leadership*, Summer 1996, 71.

5. Matt Friedeman, *The Accountability Connection* (Chicago: Victor, 1992).

6. Cited in John Maxwell, *Successful Stewardship* (El Cajon, Calif.: Injoy, 1993), 19.

7. Robert H. Schuller, *Your Church Has Real Possibilities* (Ventura, Calif.: Regal, 1974), 152–153.

8. Stan Toler, *The People Principle* (Kansas City, Mo.: Beacon Hill, 1997), 136–137.

**Chapter Eight**

1. Jim Henderson, *a.k.a. "Lost"* (Colorado Springs, Colo.: Waterbrook, 2005), 19.

2. Alan Nelson, "What's Hot (& What's Not) in Outreach," *REV!*, November/December 2007, 56.

3. Cited by Rob Wilkins, "What's Your Style?" *Moody*, May–June 1997, 13.

4. Jo Anne Lyon, *The Ultimate Blessing* (Indianapolis, Ind.: Wesleyan, 2003), 25.

5. John Kramp, "The Science of Getting Lost," *New Man*, March/April 1996, 69.

6. Fred Smith, *Learning to Lead* (Dallas: Word, 1986), 154.

7. Earle L. Wilson, *We Hold These Truths* (Indianapolis, Ind.: Wesleyan, 2000), 115.

8. Jerry Cline, Mike Slaughter, and Marc Mittelberg, "Evangelism that Flows." *Leadership*. Summer 1998, 26.

9. Tony Campolo, *Let Me Tell You a Story* (Nashville: Word, 2000), 108.

10. Stan Toler, *The People Principle* (Kansas City, Mo.: Beacon Hill, 1997), 88–90.

11. R. A. Torrey, "Saving Souls from Death," *Moody*, July/August 2000, 48.

**Chapter Nine**

1. Patricia Bolen, "Current Thoughts and Trends," *Moody*, September 1994.

2. Keith Drury, "Fourteen Reasons Why the Sunday School Has Declined," http://www.drurywriting.com/keith/ss_14.htm, accessed February 22, 2008.

3. John Koessler, "The Way to Discipleship," *Moody*, September/October 2000, 30ff.

4. Dennis Kinlaw, *The Mind of Christ* (Nappanee, Ind.: Francis Asbury Press, 1998), 68.

5. Steve DeNeff, personal communication with author, August 21, 2008.

6. Cited by Koessler.

7. Jerry Pence, "Assimilation: The Other Half of Evangelism," *Mandate*, Winter 2002, 4.

8. Keith Drury, "The Mission of the Sunday School," http://www.drurywriting.com/keith/miss_ss.htm, accessed August 20, 2008.

9. Jerry B. Jenkins, *Writing for the Soul* (Cincinnati, Ohio: Writer's Digest Books, 2006), 68–69.

**Chapter Ten**

1. Cited by Paul D. Robbins, "Comments from the Editor," *Leadership*, Fall 1980, 3.

2. Warren Bennis and Burt Nanus, *Leaders* (New York: Harper and Row, 1985), 56.

3. Hans Finzel, *The Top Ten Mistakes People Make* (Wheaton, Ill.: Victor, 1994), 52.

4. Archibald Hart, "Transference: Loosening the Tie that Blinds," in *Mastering Pastoral Counseling* (Portland, Ore.: Multnomah, 1992), 150.

5. Ibid., 151.

6. Finzel, 45.

7. Cited by Paul D. Robbins, "Comments from the Editor," *Leadership*, Fall 1980, 3.

8. Rusty Freeman, "When to Refer to a Psychiatrist," Preacher's Magazine, Sep–Nov 1997, 19–21.

9. Cited by John Maxwell and Jim Dornan, Becoming a Person of Influence (Nashville: Nelson, 1997), 90.

10. Jim Smith, "Giving Care Ethically," in *Mastering Pastoral Counseling* (Portland, Ore.: Multnomah, 1992), 32.

11. Cited by Paul D. Robbins, "Comments from the Editor," *Leadership*, Fall 1980, 3.